TOM WAITS

Other titles in the series:

Beck
The Clash
Leonard Cohen
Elvis Costello
Neil Young

TOM WAITS

Cath Carroll

THUNDER'S
MOUTH
PRESS

Published in the United States by
Thunder's Mouth Press
841 Broadway, Fourth Floor
New York, NY 10003

First published in Great Britain by Unanimous Ltd
12 The Ivories, 6–8 Northampton Street, London N1 2HY

Text editor: Ian Fitzgerald
Project editor: Nicola Birtwisle

Library of Congress Card Number: 99-69537

ISBN: 1-56025-264-2

Printed in Italy

1 2 3 4 5 6 7 8 9

CONTENTS

ACKNOWLEDGEMENTS

Special thanks to Kerry Kelekovich for assistance beyond the call of matrimony, also to David Quantick for his suggestions. Also thanks to Brian Dunn, Dan Massey, John Rice and Allen Saele, and to Simon Majumdar for his guidance. Those in search of more Waits should certainly visit the internet sites of Seth Nielsen's Tom Waits Digest, Gary Tausch's Tom Waits Miscellania and Pieter Hartmans's Tom Waits Supplement.

ONE

THE STORY

One New Year's Eve, during his early manhood, Tom Waits found himself forced to sleep in a freezing ditch somewhere off Route 66 in Arizona. The next morning, cold and dishevelled, he sought help at a small rural church nearby. It was a Sunday morning. A woman gladly took him in and allowed him to sit at the back during the Sunday service. A rickety little church band started up with music and preaching, and his hostess, a Mrs Anderson, rather inhospitably (but what an opportunity!) began to wave a demonstrative finger at the hapless Waits whenever the spoils of the devil's work were mentioned. The congregation would turn to stare at Waits, shake their heads in judgement, and then turn back to the preacher. Waits said it gave him 'a complex' and cites this episode as the inspiration for the song 'Down, Down, Down' from his 1983 album *Swordfishtrombones*.

Wherever Waits goes, a host of colourful anecdotes and tall tales swarm in his wake. The source of many such tales is the artist himself, and many are clearly not intended to be taken as serious fact. Some people have sought to define his life by assuming that if a story is repeated consistently and often, it can be assumed to be true. Using this measure, it is widely believed, and held as fact, that Tom Waits was born in the back of a taxi, or some such roving mechanism, outside Murphy Hospital in the town of Pomona, just outside of Los Angeles. It was a couple of weeks before Christmas, 7 December 1949. His parents gave the infant Thomas the very solid and functional middle name, 'Alan', and it has served him well ever since.

There are other stories and points of view that, although not repeated by the artist with great frequency, nonetheless sound very plausible, and really should be true. The Church of Shame story described above would seem to be one of those. It is certainly true for him in some reality.

And then there are the stories he just throws out there, self-contained in their own beauty and logic, and true – if only in Waits' imagination. He claims that as a child he always envied his Uncle Vernon's voice, for it was gruff and gravelly. No one ever asked Uncle Vernon to repeat anything, such was the authority of the voice. Listeners got it the first time. Waits was told the story of The Voice much later in life: following a throat operation, a small pair of scissors had been left inside Vern, forgotten by his doctors. Some time after, at a Christmas dinner with the family, and whilst choking up a string bean, Uncle Vernon had also coughed up the scissors. This had ruined his vocal cords and left him with the voice that Waits admired so much, he got one himself. Waits has commented that he thinks his own ravaged baritone suits his material. When asked if he did anything to protect his voice, he responded: 'Protect it from what? From vandals?'

Since his first released album in 1973, *Closing Time*, to his most recent, the Grammy-winning *Mule Variations* from 1999, Waits has cut thirteen original albums and written two full-length movie soundtracks, the first of which won him an Oscar nomination. He has also contributed to a startling array of other people's projects. In 1978, he took his first acting role in a feature film, and has appeared in a prestigious range of movies and plays.

His early albums are 1940s Hollywood sinister, beat hepness, drawling blues, beautiful sentimental sketches of people surprised and betrayed by their own lives yet muddling through nonetheless. Despite the close proximity of the mellow, southern California rock that dominated the Top 40 in the early 1970s, he doggedly stuck to the jazz element in his work until it might have become acceptable again, whereupon he switched to a kind of streetcorner, backwater Beefheart blues. Around this time, at the beginning of the 1980s, his attentions left the traditional set-up of piano, guitar, bass and drums, and he began incorporating musical textures from outside mainstream pop, rock and R&B, looking back to old-time carnival culture and European folklore, thus warping the context of his very American music. Writer Stephen Fried described Waits' later work as 'dwarf-ridden', which brilliantly captures the artist's move towards a Grimm fairy tale folkishness.

His audio recordings of the 1980s and '90s maintained a distinctly primitive feel. The drums were clipped, boxy and dry while around him in the mid-1980s, rock music was screaming, flanging and looming large with sumptuous stadium reverb. This didn't mean he was turning his back on the widening use of electronica, for his sonic experiments pushed the boundaries of rock further out, but miraculously, he did this without invoking the dreaded spectres of technique-heavy progressive or experimental rock. He achieved this by never leaving his base as a songwriter. He turned the musical palette of contemporary music inside out by not throwing away the past, or ignoring the future, but by sending them out on a blind date and leaving them to figure out their differences.

Theatre and rock, and indeed rock and opera, have often been dubiously paired. Waits, with his antique circus obsessions and old-time approach to music-making, has made the melding of the two forms quite seamless and quite wondrous. His songs have been hits for other people – 'Jersey Girl' (Bruce Springsteen), 'Downtown Train' (Rod Stewart), 'Strange Weather' (Marianne Faithfull), 'I Don't Want To Grow Up' (The Ramones) – but he is rarely heard on the radio and has never had a Top 40 hit himself. Says Waits, 'I seem to have a wide reputation, but my records don't sell a lot.' He muses that many people have just one album, or have heard just one and assume they know exactly what Waits is about. 'Oh, that guy. The one with the deep voice without a shave. Sings about egg and sausage ...' At the time of writing, Waits had reached the semi-finals of the 2000 Rock 'n' Roll Hall of Fame ballot. He was one of thirty-one potential nominees, with others including Gram Parsons, Black Sabbath, Dick Dale and Lou Reed. He didn't make the final shortlist of fifteen.

Not a great deal has been written about the childhood and youth of Tom Waits. When asked about it, his responses are mostly brief and self-deprecating. Best documented is his life and career in the 1970s, when the colourful jazz boho version of Waits was in progress. As with many young artists first encountering media attention, he was willing to be interviewed, and willing to talk at length, having lots of new things to say. In the 1980s, he left the bohemian image behind, split with his first manager and met his partner, Kathleen Brennan. He made fewer albums but extended his artistic scope to include several stage play collaborations. As Brennan and Waits raised their family, he seemed more inclined to protect his private life. Indeed, the life he lived at the Tropicana Motel in the 1970s was an excessively public life; if he wasn't touring, everybody knew where Tom Waits was supposed to be.

It seems that both his parents, Jesse Frank Waits and Alma Johnson McMurray, were teachers. Jesse was of Scottish-Irish descent, while Alma was partly of Norwegian stock. At the time of Waits' birth (weight: 7lb 10 oz.), they resided at 318 N Pickering Street in Whittier, California. Jesse, who is said to have been a Second World War radio technician, helped his young son build little crystal set radios, with a broom handle on the roof to serve as an antenna. The family moved around southern California until the parents' separation. His mother, he once said, sang harmony in an Andrews Sisters-style outfit. His father, a Spanish teacher, was in a Mariachi band. He related a rare boyhood anecdote to *Thrasher* magazine in 1992, regarding an unfortunate neighbour, Mr Sticha, whose front porch overlooked the town's prime skateboarding curve. Sadly Mr Sticha, a little the worse for drink (as usual), dropped dead on his porch one night. Waits and his cronies were all told they had killed him, because of their persistent skating past his house. It turned out it was an inevitable heart attack, but Waits claims it led to a lifetime of guilt and therapy.

Later in life, Waits spoke a little more of his youth. His songs' imagery would evoke, over and over, the feverish kaleidoscope of childhood memories. His father had taught Waits how to play his first guitars, $9 models that would fall apart after a couple of weeks. Jesse Waits was also fond of slipping across the border to Mexico, Waits says, where they would go to get haircuts and his father would then take him to one of the small bars. He speaks of the strange lawlessness that pervaded the area, as if it were a wild west town, saying 'it changed me'. In an interview with the film director Jim Jarmusch, he recalls images that would show up throughout the three albums that informally comprise the *Swordfishtrombones* trilogy (completed by *Rain Dogs* and *Frank's Wild Years*); oddly ancient Mexican carnivals, rides powered by car engines on wooden blocks, operated by tattooed maniacs with little respect for public safety.

It was during this conversation, with the magazine *Straight No Chaser*, that Waits revealed one of his more disturbing stories. He begins by talking of how his parents would take him to the beach in Mexico. In this story he was seven years old. At first he spoke of his father's distinctive whistle that would summon him from the water, just as it began to get too dark for safety. Having established this mood, the encroaching twilight, halfway between dark and light, between water and earth, the child still in the ocean, Waits goes on to reveal that one of these nights he saw 'a pirate ship' come out of the mist. Close enough to touch, close enough for him to see all the 'dead people' on board, before the ship sailed back into the fog. When he emerged from the water, he told his parents, who assumed, unsurprisingly, that it was a small boy's fantasy.

Waits tells a lot of stories. There was nothing about this one that made it seem any truer than, say, the Uncle Vernon and the scissors story, except that it lacks a comic element. There does seem to be a sort of mystic, visionary quality to Waits' work, one, perhaps, that he has sought to suppress at times. Just supposing the child *did* 'see' the ship, regardless of whether other people would believe it to be real, to the seven-year-old, the vision would just be another facet of reality. Jarmusch noted, without questioning the story, that visions of death ships such as this are a very common part of the pantheon of the paranormal. Later, Jarmusch and Waits talk of how Waits, encouraged by his father, would send away for radio kits. Waits swears he made contact with extra-terrestrials, that he received their signals. Unfortunately, he could not respond, for his radios were not intended for transmission.

In a different interview, with *Spin* magazine in 1994, Waits tells of another strange manifestation, a bizarre hypersensitivity to sound that tormented him around the age of fourteen. Just before he fell asleep, he would suddenly become aware of all the sounds around him, swelling in volume, 'like monsters'. 'My fingers would roar around my face... trying to make it stop.' He was terrified and convinced that soon he would die. Telling no one, he evolved meditations that would allow him to control the phenomenon. Thus began his fascination with the physical world of sound. It is no wonder that he was reluctant to confront whatever lurked in his imagination until he reached his thirties and met his wife, Kathleen Brennan, whom he has credited with encouraging him to venture more into the esoteric depths.

The Los Angeles of Waits' boyhood, between 1949 and 1959, was just emerging from the wartime boom years. The nation's munitions industry was centered there, the black jazz and R&B scene, radiating from its hub on Central Avenue, had peaked and this area was about to enter its decline. The more cerebral and, many claimed, whiter sounds of West Coast jazz were setting the scene for the 1960s California pop boom. Barney Hoskyns' enthralling history of popular music in Los Angeles, *Waiting For The Sun,* gives a detailed and vivid account of the city's cultural evolution, from strange, isolated western frontier town to strange, isolated fantasy frontier city. Waits and his family lived what seems to be a fairly standard life in the suburbs. Jesse and Alma divorced when Waits was ten, and in 1960, his mother took Tom and his two sisters south towards San Diego where they took up residence in nearby National City. Waits describes San Diego as a sailor town with the Navy being the hub of society. Most of his friends did not have fathers around. 'My dad was gone for good, and their dads were in the Philippines for eight months at a time.'

Waits did play piano as a child. Someone gave him a piano, he put it in the garage and found that he had a good ear for picking up music, even if he couldn't read it. He was not too interested in rock music, with the exception of Bob Dylan later in his teens. 'I'm just suspicious of large groups of people going anywhere together. I don't know why.' He was more taken by his parents' collection of old 78s, grooving to the hard hittin' sounds of Bing Crosby and Perry Como, acquiring an appreciation of classic Tin Pan Alley and old Hollywood-style songwriting, learning from the modern masters of this bygone era, Johnny Mercer, George Gershwin and Cole Porter. Waits' sophisticated sense of lyrical structure clearly reflects this early influence. Rather charmingly, it is alleged that he used to ask his art teacher to allow him to climb up on a table to entertain his classmates with his own interpretation of the soft-shoe shuffle.

As Waits entered his teens, he played trumpet in the high school band whilst the golden California surf sound overwhelmed pop music. As Waits matured, psychedelic folk-rock became the state religion. For pop culture fanatics around the world, the West Coast *was* the 1960s. Typically, Waits wasn't buying it: 'I wasn't thrilled by Blue Cheer, so I found an alternative... Bing Crosby.' He hadn't always been such a cynic. He has admitted that as a child, 'the radio was a pretty great thing'. With his home-made crystal set he tuned into Wolfman Jack and the evangelist Brother Springer from Oklahoma City. Thus, the larger-than-life voices, the hectoring monologists that would surface as Waits entered his thirties, began to assemble in his consciousness.

At the age of fourteen he got a job at Napoleone's pizza house in National City. Here he would work late into the night for the next five years. It was his introduction to some of the less salubrious street socialites who would populate his later songs. The job didn't do much for his school record, though. Whilst in high school, as the surf sound peaked around 1964, Waits bought a Gibson guitar and played in a band named The Systems. With typical Waits perversity, they were an R&B combo, a style of music that was, at the time, languishing in a particularly deep trough in California. As soon as biologically possible, Waits also began to cultivate a goatee, much to the derision of his boss at the pizza house. At around the age of eighteen, he discovered beat writers, absorbing the works of Jack Kerouac and Allen Ginsberg, of Charles Bukowski and of the poet Delmore Schwartz who died in the mid-1960s whilst living at a hotel for transients. Waits' obsessive residence and lifestyle at Los Angeles' Tropicana Motel was to later pay tribute to Schwartz's existence, coming uncomfortably close to repeating it.

The young Waits began subscribing to *Down Beat* magazine. It's 1967 and the rest of America is voyaging through a tangerine cosmos, guitar solos are getting way out of hand, and body paint is giving the garment trade pause for thought. Waits still has the goatee and has taken to wearing dark glasses. 'It's just like when you buy a record and you hold it under your arm and make sure everyone can see the title of it. It's about identity.' He found himself enthralled by the insidious musicality of the beat poets' bare words. He began fashioning his own songs which were, by his own description, parodies of existing songs with the substitution of obscene lyrics. Of this time he has said that he hadn't considered a career in music, his ambitions lay more in the restaurant business, hoping that he might one day buy into a place. When it came to music, 'I was a patron, no more no less.'

The facts surrounding his entry into performing are some-what hazy. At some point, he held a job as a doorman at the Heritage club in Los Angeles, which is sadly no more. There he was exposed to a broad range of music, such as jazz, rock and folk. Somewhere along the line, Waits began performing him-self. Inspired by Bob Dylan's masterful fusion of music and sto-rytelling, supposedly living out of his car, travelling up to LA to play at the Troubadour Club's famous open evenings, Waits doggedly plied his trade until he came to the attention of one Herb Cohen, who became his manager.

So, somewhere along the line, between Napoleone's pizza house and the Troubadour, Waits found himself an effective writing process; he began noting down the conversations he heard around him at the bar of the San Diego club where he worked. 'I found some music hiding in there.' He has said that in doing this, he hoped to make something meaningful out of the frequently unhappy and vulnerable lives he came upon, to give this sadness in the human condition some dignity. This underlying melancholy, verging on a tenderness, is something that runs deep in his work. Rather delightfully he later said 'I just try to steer a course between the pomp and the piss.' He has always underplayed his exposure to conventional literature at this point. By the time he first auditioned at the Troubadour, in 1969, he has claimed his reading matter was 'limited to menus and magazines', although he does concede 'I really start-ed to shine after school.' In June 1971, Herb Cohen saw Waits playing at a hoot night and proposed that they work together.

The famed Troubadour club at 9081 Santa Monica Boulevard in Hollywood, which began as a folk club run by owner Doug Weston, was approaching its third decade of host-ing live music. It acquired a reputation for diversity (and today, it's a metal hangout), and was considered the most prestigious place to play in LA. It was the setting for countless artists' showcases as they courted the assembled nobility of the music business. It is even credited with being the birthplace of country rock, being the spawning ground for many of the superstars of the era, The Eagles, Jackson Browne and Linda Ronstadt. It was here that Waits' performance was noticed by Cohen. At the time, Waits considered this a much wished-for piece of good fortune, albeit rather daunting, for it meant that someone else took his career as a songwriter seriously. Cohen was an established member of the LA rock community. He had operated a folk club, The Unicorn, and had gone on to manage Frank Zappa and Linda Ronstadt. Around 1976, Waits said of this offer, 'You just have to take it, along with the responsibility.'

Herb Cohen had entered into a creative and business partnership with avant-garde rock orchestrator, the late Frank Zappa, some years prior, when they formed Straight Records together, a sister company to Zappa's Bizarre Productions. Straight went on to release a host of critically noted but commercially indigestible albums from a variety of West Coast eccentrics and post-psychedelic pioneers. These included Jerry Yester & Judy Henske's *Farewell Aldebaran*, Wild Man Fischer's *An Evening With Wild Man Fischer* and the late Tim Buckley's more outtasight jazz-folk meanderings. Probably the most celebrated release, apart from Zappa's own extravaganzas, was Captain Beefheart and his Magic Band's 1969 album *Trout Mask Replica*, which turned traditional rock-blues into a disjointed, absurdist patois. It was released in the same year that Jack Kerouac died. Somewhat amusingly, it has been rumoured that the rather offbeat Beefheart was somewhat vexed by his suspicion that Zappa was passing him off as yet another of the Bizarre Empire Freaks. This would have been quite a feat of inverse salesmanship, since Beefheart (born Don

Van Vliet) composed music whose calculated complexity and sophistication was self-evident. The improvisations of Larry 'Wild Man' Fischer and the chaotic exuberance of groupie trio the GTOs were clearly a different kind of art. Cohen later had an acrimonious dispute with Zappa in the late 1970s. Cohen and Waits went on to have some legal disputes of their own in the early to mid-1990s. Commerce and art, often so necessarily intertwined, have caused endless heartache and misery, as thousands of other artists and their business associates will attest. Cohen was at the centre of one of rock's most colourful communities, although his contribution has not always been appreciated. Pamela Des Barres, the self-confessed über-groupie and Zappa satellite, once indignantly remarked that Cohen wasn't eccentric at all, and that he just 'just stood around scowling'.

Encouraged by Cohen, Waits moved to Los Angeles and between July and September 1971 Waits recorded a number of original songs, later to be the cause of a legal battle between the two when Cohen decided to release the demos in two volumes under the title *The Early Years*.

The first volume featured four songs that later appeared on Waits albums, and nine songs that didn't. Of these hitherto-unreleased nine, it would be hard to find a persuasive argument for their inclusion, except as historical artifact. We can assume that the songs, recorded when Waits was only twenty-two, represent his very first attempts at writing. It was the material sold as the second volume that surely must have convinced David Geffen to sign the young man to his Asylum label. Most of these songs were later re-recorded, and they show a musical maturity beyond Waits' years. The voice is significantly different, mostly a boyish whine with a little blues in it, somewhere between Don Henley of The Eagles and Eric Clapton. He commented that he was fortunate in coming up as a songwriter at a time when the perception of songwriters as a faceless Brill-Building production line was changing for good. Until then, 'Nobody made a distinction between a song Elvis sang and a song Elvis wrote. Did he write it? Does it matter? No.'

Financially bolstered by his income from singer-songwriter Laura Nyro's publishing catalogue, David Geffen founded Asylum Records in 1970. In 1971, it was added to the Warners empire, which included the folk-rock champion label, Elektra. Geffen remained Asylum president and the label became home to the royalty of southern California rock, The Eagles, Joni Mitchell, Jackson Browne and Linda Ronstadt. Geffen became head of the newly combined Asylum-Elektra in 1973, when Elektra's previous president, Jac Holzman, retired. Geffen left Elektra-Asylum when he sold out his share in 1975, whereupon industry wit and super emcee Joe Smith took over. Waits was not exactly Smith's cup of tea. When Smith heard the demos for *Swordfishtrombones* in 1982 he decided it was time for Waits to part company with the label, and the singer signed to Island Records.

The early 1970s was the start of Waits' infamous residency at the Tropicana Motel in West Hollywood. Residency as in he lived there. The Trop (demolished in 1987) stood at 8585 Santa Monica Boulevard, and was owned by the ex-baseball star Sandy Koufax. It had become the west coast equivalent of the Chelsea Hotel, the legendary New York rock 'n' roll hang-out which first achieved notoriety in the 1960s. One of the Chelsea Hotel's favourite sons, Andy Warhol, used The Tropicana as a location in his movie *Heat*. Waits says he paid around $9 per night for the privilege of living there. His pal, Rickie Lee Jones, more or less lived there with him, and later on, a hard-living romance bloomed. With the help of their tireless friend Chuck

E Weiss, a fairly debauched time was had by all. Interviewers seeking Waits out noted that his kitchen served only to house his piano. Waits didn't use the refrigerator and considered the stove to be just a 'large cigarette lighter'. He has maintained that eventually the lifestyle – and his very public address – became overwhelming and he had to move on. He cites the symbolism of the motel's swimming pool being painted black as the last straw. As Barney Hoskyns has noted, others maintain that the pool simply turned black from all the lawn furniture thrown into it by the twenty-four-hour rock 'n' roll party people. Waits did not seem too bothered about amassing a rock fortune, although naturally, he had his modest bills to pay and, when cash permitted, had his own musicians to water and feed. Rather touchingly, he admitted that 'I want my old man to think that what I'm doing is good.'

It was Herb Cohen's idea that Waits should take his act on tour with Frank Zappa and his band, The Mothers of Invention. Cohen managed Zappa and convinced Waits that he should take advantage of the opportunity to work up a stage act and, as it turned out, a thick skin. Waits went on tour with Zappa over the next two years, from November 1973 until the summer of 1975, whenever the chance presented itself. Another Herb Cohen client, Tim Buckley, had been Zappa's opening act prior to this. It was reported he did not have much fun, for Zappa's devoted fans were a tough audience to please. Waits found little had changed. He first met Zappa in Canada in the autumn of 1973. Waits has said he was somewhat intimidated by Zappa because of the legend that surrounded him. Zappa was a charismatic man of fierce intelligence and vision, and Waits claimed he used him, the opening act, as some kind of rectal thermometer to gauge the audience's mood. Waits was probably as good as any other opening act since the Mothers and Zappa had no equivalent, at least on this planet, and it helped that Waits was a bit of an oddity too. Waits told Barney Hoskyns, writing for *Mojo* magazine in 1999, that he still had bad dreams about the tours: 'Frank shows up asking how the audience were... ' He has also commented that the only reason the audience didn't hurt him was because Frank Zappa was there, keeping 'his people' in check. Of his live performances around this time, Waits has commented, 'I didn't know what the hell I was doing.' There seemed to be little in the way of conscious career strategy. This rather brutalizing experience didn't deter the young songwriter from following his own path.

There are several Zappa bootlegs from this era that archive a small portion of Waits and Zappa interacting at one live show. Waits has finished his act, playing solo at the piano, the audience hadn't really cared for him (cries of 'You SUCK!') and Zappa has been on stage a while. The Mothers strike up the musical backing to 'Ol' 55' and Zappa asks where 'The Wino' is, speculating that he was probably backstage drinking (Zappa himself maintained a resolutely sober and drug-free lifestyle). Waits obligingly appears and relates a couple of well-told but low-end jokes. The first is a whimsical, vulgar and profoundly libellous joke about three of America's favourite country singers, to which the punchline is 'They'd never seen six inches of snow in June before.' It wasn't really the kind of experimental, art-lab humour that Zappa's audience would have appreciated, which was probably of some comfort to young Tom. The other anecdote has achieved semi-legendary status amongst Waits' 'people', where it is known as the Twelve Inch joke. Here it is in unadorned form, for no one can tell it like Tom: a man stops at a bar and out of his pocket jumps a very annoying little man. Despite being just twelve inches tall, the tiny fellow wrecks the bar and everyone hates him. When asked to account for his pint-sized companion, the larger of the two men confesses that he met a genie who offered to grant him whatever he wished for, which turned out to be a twelve-inch prick. Maybe Zappa's audience weren't so wrong after all...

In 1973, Waits was sent into Sunset Sound recording studio in Hollywood, and with the aid of producer Jerry Yester taped the twelve songs that appear as his first album, *Closing Time*, released later that year. The sleeve depicts a youthful, earnest Waits, with an inordinate amount of hair, although it could not be described as long in a hippyish way. By now, the goatee has fully matured. Slumped over a piano, he is modelling his trademark fashion, a scruffy variation on the 1930s working man. A collarless white shirt, sleeves rolled up, old, black vest. Although the lighting in the photo cuts him off at the waist, we can assume he's wearing pants, the usual, old, black and narrow. It is a style that has worn very well on him, and, presumably, saved him an awful lot of time figuring out what to wear in the morning (or late afternoon, as it probably was, when he got up). Occasionally, he might top the ensemble with a grubby 1920s newsboy cap, or in later years, a First World War helmet. Without straying into the dangerous territory of costume (quite an achievement in the 1970s), he managed to establish a personal style that affirmed his old-time roots and hobo affiliation whilst transcending fashion.

The album's producer, Jerry Yester, was a mainstay of the LA folk-rock scene and was the ex-husband of the somewhat cultish folk singer Judy Henske (another Herb Cohen client). Yester had been a member of the Modern Folk Quartet and was also in a later incarnation of the Lovin' Spoonful. Despite working in the folk-rock field, he was a self-described 'beatnik', even during the hippie era. With his former wife Judy, they released the almost indescribable experimental album, *Farewell*

Aldebaran, a work which was deemed loopy enough to be given the Zappa seal of approval. This obscure recording included a lot of electronic experimentation mixed in with pop, pre-Goth dronings and olde-worlde folk. After this oddity, Yester went off to work with Pat Boone. He was what you'd call an open-minded fellow.

Waits has commented that *Closing Time* would have ended up as a folk album if he hadn't supervised it so much. The artist also admits that at the time, lack of experience meant he could not articulate how he heard the songs in his head. He would, in retrospect, have liked to have had a little more jazz and fewer strings. For the listener, this may not be so much of an issue. It is a wonderfully crafted collection of songs, rendered with just enough edge to take the pink tones out of the sentimental parts. Tim Buckley later did a glorious Jimmy-Webb-meets-Glenn-Campbell's-string-section version of 'Martha' and The Eagles took 'Ol' 55' and made it into a freeway anthem. Not a bad beginning for a twenty-four-year-old, who five years previously had not really considered music as a way of life.

Waits may not have cared much for their treatment of his work, but it did show that he could write for the pop world. The album was well-received critically, but soon disappeared from the public's radar. As Waits continued to wear the hair shirt that touring with Zappa represented, he began to find his voice. The next album, recorded in July 1974, *The Heart Of Saturday Night,* was to mark an important transition, although not one that reflected the way popular music was going at the time. This time, there was a new producer, one with an even deeper pedigree than Yester.

By the time Bones Howe went to work with Waits, he had a formidable reputation as a versatile engineer, having come up through the ranks of the LA jazz scene in the 1950s. After this he worked as engineer and producer for several West Coast pop acts, including the Association, Fifth Dimension and The Mamas and The Papas. David Geffen had introduced Howe to the young songwriter, noting that Waits had strong beat and jazz shadings in his work that had not been brought out on *Closing Time*. After meeting Waits, Howe noted that Waits was the first artist from his generation who knew about the same things Howe did. Waits, for his part, was impressed by Howe's history: 'He loves the mythology of the music scene. He'll say, "I stood right here with Elvis Presley."' It was to be the beginning of a seven-album partnership, giving Waits a solid schooling in engineering and production, and establishing an anchored foundation from which the artist could plot the boundaries of his musical vocabulary.

Lyrically, the album was a significant step forward. The rather sweet conventions of *Closing Time* were a fading thing, but some of the 1970s piano man still remained in songs like 'Shiver Me Timbers' and 'San Diego Serenade'. However, Mancini-esque sax solos began slinking through the songs, adding a strange retro glamour. Waits finally gets to pay tribute to his beatnik heroes with the surprisingly mature and colourful 'Diamonds On My Windshield', a rhythmic piece of storytelling inspired by performer and writer Ken Nordine's spoken-word jazz. Bones Howe has commented that *The Heart Of Saturday Night* was probably the most 'produced' album the two ever put together, since he felt Waits needed to distinctly dissociate himself from the earnest singer-songwriter vibe of the previous album. To emphasize the break, Mike Melvoin, who had previously worked alongside the core of musicians known as The Wrecking Crew, used by Phil Spector, was brought in as an arranger.

This new approach to the lyrical content of the song, where there seemed to be more fiction in the first-person characters voicing the songs, has caused much controversy regarding where the real Tom Waits begins and ends. Many of his interviews have moments when he seems to disappear inside another voice, spinning tales, riffing on the nonsensical and generally seeming a little diffident about the answer. He shrugs it off, saying, 'People just want to be told something they don't already know.' Waits is clearly a thoughtful, compassionate and highly intelligent individual, even at the peak of his Tropicana posturing, and it's hard to believe that these characters didn't draw some of their essential life force from their creator. Interestingly, his former girlfriend, Rickie Lee Jones, when interviewed for a documentary, said of Waits, 'he knew when to be eccentric, which was nice.' That Waits is genuinely eccentric there is no doubt, that there is an element of his eccentric personality that he can turn off and on for the media and for his own creative processes, there should be no doubt either.

Rickie Lee Jones, herself a songwriter with a beat fixation, was Waits' companion throughout the mid-1970s. They met and clicked because they were the only two people at the denim-swamped Troubadour who liked *West Side Story* (this was 1975, pre-Gap commercials). According to legend, they would greet each other with finger-snappin' renditions of 'When you're a Jet... ' Not only was Jones hip to Waits' secret record collection, but she could also keep up with his drinking. Rickie Lee was described as a streetwise party urchin when she arrived in LA following a teenage life of travelling around the west coast. It was 1973 and she was just nineteen years old. She subsidized her existence by waitressing, and played her songs to whomever would listen. One person who eventually did was Little Feat's frontman, Lowell George, who immediately asked to include her 'Easy Money' on his solo album *Thanks I'll Eat It Here*. This was not until 1978, however, when she was signed to Warners and had been given the opportunity to record her first album, *Rickie Lee Jones*. In May 1979, she had a US Top Five hit with 'Chuck E's in Love', a song about who else but Tropicana hang-out buddy and sometime singer-songwriter Chuck E Weiss. This hit gave her more exposure than Waits had ever had with his slow-burning career. Unhappily, however, Rickie Lee's tempestuous and difficult early days set the scene for many years of struggling with alcohol and life itself.

Like Waits, Jones had an uncompromising grip on her artistic vision. She was bold enough to dismiss the Queen of Everything, Joni Mitchell, as a jazz carpetbagger and to assert that she, Jones, was the one leading the true Jazz Life, out there on the edge. All of her albums, *Rickie Lee Jones* (1979), *Pirates* (1981), *Girl At Her Volcano* (1983), featuring the song 'Rainbow Sleeves' which Waits wrote but never recorded himself, and *Magazine* (1984), testified to her luminous talent even though her career remained a carefully-tended cult item. In 1989 Steely Dan's Walter Becker and Scottish band The Blue Nile worked with her to produce *Flying Cowboys*. This and her follow-up album, *Pop Pop*, contain jazz interpretations of a broad spectrum of popular song and served to remind the world of her achievements. The previously noted documentary, *Naked Songs*, was an account of the acoustic tour she undertook after releasing her 1993 album, *Traffic From Paradise*. Around this time, a new breed of 1990s female singer-songwriter was paying homage to Jones' influence, twenty years after she first took to the stage of The Troubadour.

The Rocky Mountain city of Denver can be thanked for bringing us another of Waits' constant companions at The Tropicana, the exotic enigma that is Chuck E Weiss, who was to be Waits' best buddy throughout the Tropicana years. The son of a record-loving salvage man, his taste in music was truly eclectic. Chuck E was another of those characters that one would assume was a figment of Waits' imaginings. But no. The young Weiss found himself especially taken by the blues and found himself most at home behind a drum kit. As a teenager, he got his break filling in as a last-minute sub for Lightnin' Hopkins, the grizzled blues giant. The gig turned into a new career for Weiss, who backed a number of blues and roots musicians throughout the late 1960s. Waits and Weiss supposedly first met in 1972 in a coffee shop next door to a Denver nightclub, where Waits was due to perform. At the time, Weiss's personal style was more in keeping with the fashions of the blues circuit he played. Although he claims to have mistaken the beatnik troubadour Waits for some 'old bum', the two began a musical and personal friendship that endures to this day. Weiss apparently moved to Los Angeles in 1975, where he, Waits and Rickie Lee Jones created no end of trouble.

Waits produced Weiss's 1999 album *Extremely Cool*, contributing two duets, one of which was 'Do You Know What I Idi Amin'. One might guess that being around these two, at times, would be rather wearing. Weiss co-wrote the song 'Spare Parts' which appears on *Nighthawks At The Diner*. The colourful sideman didn't release an album himself until 1981, when a collection of his demos came out under the title *The Other Side Of Town*. He remained a popular attraction on the LA scene and his band The Goddamn Liars became the house act at Johnny Depp's ultra-trendy Viper Room club.

In 1975, Waits was still touring with Zappa. By this time his ego had developed the necessary callouses that would help buffer him from the critical backlash that greeted his next album, *Nighthawks At The Diner*. This was the same year that Bruce Springsteen had released *Born To Run*. Waits had seen him play and was quite bowled over by the New Jersey roaring man. Of course, you wouldn't know this from checking out *Nighthawks*. It was a double album, recorded live in front of an invited audience at the Record Plant in LA. Bones Howe returned, this time with a jazz quartet, and Waits played the beat-blueshound and late-night conversationalist. The album didn't do a thing to further his career at the time, nobody seemed to like it, although in retrospect it adds a pleasing depth and authenticity to his back catalogue. Given the state of music and of Waits' career at the time, releasing *Nighthawks* was a far bolder move than the mainstream release in 1993 of the teutonic toe-tapper *Black Rider*.

The Waits voice starts to get that ridiculous gruff sound around this period. The phlegmy old scat singer shuffles up, lisping and chortling, 'a-heh-heh-heh', winking at the audience, pontificating and admitting, whilst in character, to asking himself out on a date and then taking advantage of himself, 'making the scene with a magazine, uh-heh-heh', which impresses his audience no end. He stresses, to their obvious delight, that he's 'not weird about it... I don't tie myself up first.' This monologue, preceding 'Better Off Without A Wife', is a prime example of Waits' skill as an after-hours, charmingly blue raconteur. His repartee bears more than a trace of the American cult hero Richard 'Lord' Buckley, whose comedic jazz-improv verbalizations had so impressed the young Lenny Bruce. Coincidentally, Frank Zappa had made it his business in the mid-1960s to acquire the rights to many of Lord Buckley's recordings. His Lordship had sadly passed away some fifteen years previous to the release of *Nighthawks*. One point of note is that Waits sounds a lot more cheerful and friendly than some of the concert reviews of the time seemed to suggest.

Waits was still earning next to nothing as an opening act and could not afford to keep up a regular backing trio. He toured solo, building up his status as a lone performer. He speaks of an uncomfortable residency at the swanky Manhattan club, the Reno Sweeney. He then opened for country-rock stars Poco in Passaic, New Jersey, where the hostile audience gave the Zappa crowd a run for their money. Waits' astounding resilience was beginning to crack under the strain of unsympathetic audiences, too much backstage drinking and lots of bad food ingested at irregular intervals. It was the usual life of a touring musician. Things improved somewhat in December 1975, when *Rolling Stone*'s Jon Landau gave Waits a dazzling review. In January 1976, he taped an appearance on *Soundstage* before an appreciative Chicago audience, and a month later, appeared on *The Dinah Shore Show*. Ms Shore was a little less hip to Waits' Beat demeanour, but he went ahead and sang 'Warm Beer And Cold Women' anyway. But just around the corner was a crushing experience in New Orleans that would, in a roundabout way, lead to his breakthrough album of 1976, *Small Change*.

This album was written after Waits quit touring in the USA in disgust after some celebrity members of Bob Dylan's entourage (whom Waits christened 'The Rolling Blunder Revue') took over the stage in a New Orleans club, just an hour before Waits himself was due to begin his lonely act. Nobody had consulted, or even warned him. The ensuing tambourine-flapping celebrity jam included Roger McGuinn (formerly of The Byrds), Joan Baez (top folkie-activist), and Kinky Friedman (your average Jewish, satirical country singer and author). Waits was having a hard enough time appealing to the audience as it was. When he took to the stage, the audience was in no mood to give their attention to the quirky, not-very-famous character at the piano, they were too busy looking around the room for higher-wattage celebrities. This was the final straw and Waits stumped off to Europe where he spent two weeks in London.

This gave him the time and the solitude he had been missing for years. In an astonishing act of creativity, he put together twenty songs and selected eleven of these gems for his masterpiece fourth album, *Small Change*. There is little room for the sunny side of the street on this collection, but beneath the cynical grit and keen observations, there is a grim empathetic, humanistic humour. At this time, Waits made his debut appearance at the famed London jazz club Ronnie Scott's, where it is said he played to a fairly empty house for three nights. They threw him out on night four. 'I think it was my clothes,' said Waits. He also made an appearance on the British TV rock show *The Old Grey Whistle Test*. Waits took advantage of the geographical proximity and briefly toured Scandinavia and the Benelux countries at the same time, where he found a warmer and more appreciative audience.

The trusty Bones Howe produced *Small Change* and, with Waits' encouragement, the album was recorded live to two-track, just as Howe would do with his jazz acts back in the 1950s. The result was one of Waits' best records, and for those who prefer their Waits seen through the bottom of a glass, the essential album. Many of the LP's songs remained in Waits' live performances for years to come and he would often end the evening with the agonizingly sad 'Tom Traubert's Blues', with its weary 'Waltzing Matilda' refrain. Participating musicians included the late Shelly Manne, a celebrated LA jazz drummer. Manne once said of Waits, 'He's kind of an anachronism, isn't he?' Lew Tabackin added saxophone and Jim Hughart played bass. The title track, 'Small Change', chronicles, in heartbreakingly realistic detail, the premature and violent death of a smalltime street punk, killed in the street with his own gun. Waits paints a pitifully matter-of-fact picture of a wasted life, and at a fundraiser for a crime-racked Los Angeles almost twenty years later, he opened with this song and its resonance proved timeless.

Another favourite that has stood the test of time is 'Pasties And A G-String', a beat rap set to a relentless jazz shuffle, that effortlessly lent itself to a modern rap interpretation when Jeffrey Lee Pierce of The Gun Club reworked the song for the Waits tribute album *Step Right Up*. This ode to burlesque shows is a rare excursion into the land of lascivious song (if you ignore the raunchy patter on *Nighthawks*, as millions of record buyers did). Waits is not shy about paying his respects to the lovely ladies, but he usually does so with a sweep of longing and, often, regret. But not here. The song's protagonist, whilst watching the jiggling flesh of the floorshow, is rendered 'harder than Chinese algebra', after which, there is really nowhere else to go. Another insistent song-poem, 'Step Right Up', is Waits' comment on the state of the music business. He said of the song, in which a huckster sells off goods, faulty and otherwise, at bargain-basement prices, that he chose to write the song rather than submit a formal essay on the state of consumer vulnerability to *Scientific American*. Too bad, he should have done both. The lyric sheet on the album cover omits the printed lyrics to this song. Instead, Waits sets record buyers a challenge, writing on the sleeve notes: 'For the lyrics to "Step Right Up" send by prepaid mail a photo of yourself, two dead creeping charlies, and a self-addressed stamped envelope to: The Tropicana Motor Hotel, Hollywood, California c/o Young Tom Waits. Please allow 30 days for delivery.'

Waits has long had a somewhat ambivalent attitude to the process of music product and its promotion. *Small Change* was a hit and as a result Waits found himself touring constantly and having to account for himself in public. Naturally, the better his albums sold, the more he was treated like a commodity. Step right up, indeed. An interview with *Playboy* over ten years later had him talking into a tape recorder for fear of being misquoted – whereupon he announced that, from time to time, he would 'pull [the] string' of the reporter. A typical Waits conundrum. In 1975, Waits had stated that he was more preoccupied with where he would be in ten years than where he would be within twelve months. Although hailed as the new Bob Dylan by an enthusiastic press, Waits seemed to understand that, if he were to be faithful to his muse, he would not be gracing the Top 10 in the nearish future. For a start, his backing musicians, sometimes calling themselves the Nocturnal Emissions, would have to do something about their name.

The mid-to-late 1970s saw much of the Los Angeles music business willingly surrendering to the avalanche of cocaine and associated indulgences that nearly killed many of its royalty. Waits himself was not one of the Canyon party people, but the climate surrounding the increased momentum of his career, and all the partying and attention that went with it, gave him pause. Around about this time, he started to reconsider the attraction of drinking, considering that perhaps it was not romantic nor was it essential for the creation of art. In 1985 he told the *NME*'s Gavin Martin, 'I don't want to romanticize liquor to the point of ridiculousness.' Nine years previously, he told *Rolling Stone* that he had really spent time crafting *Small Change*'s 'Bad Liver And A Broken Heart'. He had ceased to believe that there was anything amusing or even American about a drunk, and had realized that all his writing about the subject had only convinced his audience that Waits himself was booked with a one-way ticket on the old cirrhosis express. He wrote the song mostly for the benefit of those people. 'I started telling myself to cut that shit out', he said, and by the time his last album on Elektra was released, he pretty much had. He'd stopped smoking and confined himself to the occasional tipple of red wine. The smoking cessation was a serious break from the image of yore, for one would be challenged to find a photograph of him in the first third of his career where he isn't smoking and doesn't have couple of packs of Viceroys stuffed into his pockets and waistband.

It seems quite plausible that the whole hard-living lifestyle may have been, at first, maintained as a kind of method acting approach to writing – for Waits had not considered himself a writer until he was in his twenties, and perhaps didn't have any writing process in place to rely on. And, although he, a nice-looking, middle-class boy from a suburban home, willingly elected to live the rather sleazy, transient existence at the Tropicana, he must have also felt the despair of the place start to set in. There is a point, albeit hard to define for the sightseeing drinker, when he or she loses their tourist status and becomes simply a drunk. Waits was certainly in danger of painting himself into the picture he was creating.

Duke's Tropicana coffee shop, pictured for the curious on the front cover of the *Step Right Up* tribute album, was the scene of an altercation in late May 1977, when Waits and Chuck E were arrested for disturbing the peace. The two later filed a successful complaint against the Los Angeles sheriff's office. During the arrest, the two men were handcuffed and held at gunpoint. Three plainclothes officers had been involved in a scuffle with another Duke's customer and, according to reports, Tom and Chuck had first gone to this customer's assistance, and then left the diner. The officers followed them, identified themselves, and, misinterpreting Weiss's sudden movement, forcibly restrained the two. Tom and Chuck were described as being accompanied by an 'unidentified female companion', who we would all like to believe was Rickie Lee, just to complete a perfect picture. According to Herb Cohen's statement to *Rolling Stone*, the men were told they were being arrested for homosexual soliciting, amongst other things. Eyewitness accounts assured that the boisterous twosome were acquitted of all charges. Waits was heard to complain that the officers had recycled too many *Dragnet* clichés.

Just prior to the Duke's coffee shop altercation, Waits had played in Europe and, whilst in Amsterdam in April of that year, the photographs were taken that were used for the artwork of the later *The Early Years* collection. At the end of July, he and Bones Howe went back into the studio to record *Foreign Affairs*, on which Waits and Bette Midler duet on 'I Never Talk To Strangers' to great effect. Midler had already covered 'Shiver Me Timbers' the previous year. The themes established in *Small Change* were largely continued, with the exception of the lovely 'Potter's Field' and the startling 'Burma Shave'.

Once again, Waits toured to promote the album, and this time he hired strippers to open the show. By now he could afford a trio again, and because his band mates protested against Tom's habit of staying in flophouses, Waits improved his choice of accommodation too. Having lived the street life for a good five years, he had very much established his personal style and could afford to upgrade a little without fear of being branded bourgeois. He toured the US throughout the autumn and winter, and at the end of November was profiled in *Time* magazine. Waits also began to broaden his artistic range after being asked to contribute to and appear in the film *Paradise Alley* with a pre-Rambo Sylvester Stallone. Waits' first movie role was a small one, as Mumbles the piano player. His later comments about this job suggest that it was financial need that motivated his appearance. However, he did have standards to maintain: he was also asked to appear as a satanic cult leader on the hugely popular TV cop show, *Starsky And Hutch*, but Waits, somewhat insulted, turned down the opportunity.

Meanwhile, the big wheels of rock kept a-turnin' and Waits soon found himself back in a Hollywood recording studio in August 1978, recording *Blue Valentine*. Trivia fans please note that the blonde leaning back over the car with Waits is Rickie Lee Jones. The album was released in autumn 1978, around the same time that the soundtrack to *Paradise Alley* was released, which featured two Waits originals, the concert favourite 'Annie's Back In Town' and 'Paradise Alley'. The rest of the year was spent playing concerts across north America. The following year, Rickie Lee Jones had her first album released and found herself with a hit single. Waits continued his live work, visiting Australia in March. But by late autumn of that year, his romantic relationship with Jones was over and he left LA for New York.

Waits spent the first few months of 1980 in New York, hoping the experience of a new environment would reveal new perspectives in his art and help him break away from the life he had been living. He has told a couple of publications that he even took fitness classes, although his attitude wasn't quite there. He tells of running to a class with a cigarette in one hand and an alcoholic drink in the other (the container was foil-covered, so as not to spill). A lovely image, regardless of its veracity. The 1980s were to mark a significant change in Waits' work, one which brought a great deal of critical respect. He has said the change in the 1980s was the result of a hundred little decisions as he reached the end of a cycle. One big change that year was his marriage. Whilst working on *Paradise Alley*, Waits had met Kathleen Brennan, a writer and artist, who was employed as a script editor at Francis Ford Coppola's Zoetrope film studio. She was to be Waits' future partner in life and art and represents, more than anything, the reason the change in the singer's work was so profound and so long-lasting.

When first in New York, Waits had encountered film director Francis Ford Coppola and began discussing the possibility of working on a full-length feature film soundtrack at Coppola's Zoetrope empire. When Waits returned to LA, they made the deal and Waits got his very own office to work in. He even got memos. For some time he had harboured a Brill Building fantasy in which he got to write to a schedule, and didn't depend on the slow-fermenting, entirely subjective approach he had always relied on previously. It wasn't the first time Waits had been offered a full-length film to score, but this was the first time he'd felt he was really the right person for the task.

When Coppola first told him the movie he had in mind was going to be a 'lounge operetta', Waits was at first a little dismayed and he thought to himself, 'well, you're a couple of years too late.' Despite this, the project – which was eventually revealed to be the movie *One From The Heart* – appealed to him so he went ahead. However, he found that a change is not always a good thing, especially when you also have to change other peoples' ideas about your work. In mid June, Waits took a month-and-a-half break and he and Bones Howe booked themselves into the Filmways/Heider Studio B in Hollywood to record *Heartattack And Vine*. His first producer, Jerry Yester, was to return to add some string arrangements on the sweetheart song 'Jersey Girl'. The Captain Beefheart influence that grew in Waits' work over the next few years creeps in on this album, and it was to be Howe's penultimate production. Waits was to find that the only way to make a complete change of style was to start afresh with different personnel, though here he starts to push towards that new way of working. Before he started work on the album Waits had thought about using a new producer, considering at one point the starmaker-arranger-producer Jack Nitzsche (who spent many years working along-side the alarming Phil Spector). Eventually, Waits decided to stick with Howe, sensing he would would feel more comfortable taking risks in his presence.

The track 'Downtown' contains a reference to a certain Montclaire de Havelin doing the St Vitus dance. This is apparently a pseudonym used by Waits when overnighting at hotels, in order to avoid unwelcome visitors. The title track, 'Heartattack And Vine', has a background of pitiful whimsy, as one might expect. Our hero was in a bar on Hollywood Boulevard, close to Vine Street, when a homeless woman carrying a dead animal stepped up to the bar and told the bartender she was going to have a heart attack. 'Yeah, well have it outside' was the kindly innkeeper's response. Waits thought this rather 'chilly', and renamed the boulevard forever.

A significant addition to the album was a re-recording of the song 'On The Nickel', which had originally been tracked as the title song to a Ralph Waites documentary about a couple of old friends who first met on skid row in LA. One of them was still there, 'on the nickel', as they termed it. The album also contained the lovely, perennial, 'Ruby's Arms', a terribly sad, too-early-in-the-morning goodbye song. A vintage cast of musicians joined Waits and Howe for this venture. Amongst them were Canned Heat's bassist Larry Taylor, New Orleans keyboard legend and Dr John cohort Ronnie Baron, and Angelino Roland Bautista playing guitar. Another Dr John sideman, 'Big John' Thomassie, played drums. Thomassie had been part of Waits' road band for the past two years and this was his first recording. Bob Alcivar, who assisted with *Foreign Affairs*, returned to add his expertise to 'On The Nickel' and 'Saving All My Love

For You'. Waits' soon-to-be longtime collaborator Greg Cohen also played bass. Symbolically absent from the credits was any mention of Chuck E Weiss, a metaphor for the break with his LA past.

The methodical approach to songwriting that Waits had to take when working on *One From The Heart* was utilized in a somewhat compressed fashion in making *Heartattack*. Waits says he actually moved into the recording studio, situated in the old RCA building at Ivar and Sunset, and wrote there, staying one song ahead of the band, and found the faster approach to writing to be gruelling but invigorating.

For those who have examined the album's mock newspaper front page cover, and have wondered who David 'Doc' Feuer might be, since his name and phone number are scribbled in one corner, Waits claims he is a New York psychiatrist who 'needed the work'. This wasn't much of a favour, since the number was entirely fictional, but doubtless the very real Dr Feuer was probably quite relieved by this fact.

Instead of going back on the road, Waits went back to Zoetrope, where the experience of writing for someone else's approval had been a valuable lesson. That the other person was Francis Ford Coppola, a man renowned for his inexhaustible ability to oversee a project, made the situation all the more instructive. They obviously got along, for Waits went on to work on other film projects with Coppola. For *One From The Heart*, Waits maintained a two-room office on the former Hollywood general lot that housed Coppola's kingdom, with a window overlooking (what else?) Santa Monica boulevard. A reporter found him there, still wearing the roach-impaler shoes and the old black suit, with the floor awash with notebooks and cassettes. It was to be an eighteen-month project and was a welcome relief from the endless album-tour-album-tour treadmill.

Heartattack And Vine was released shortly after Waits' marriage to Kathleen. They were later to honeymoon in Tralee, the Irish town immortalized in the old Irish folk song 'The Rose of Tralee'. Waits has alleged that Kathleen won his heart with her ability to lie on a bed of nails, 'stick a knitting needle through her lip and still drink coffee'. And we wonder why she doesn't make many public appearances? Waits has explained of his wife: 'She doesn't like the limelight, but she's an incandescent presence on all songs we work on together.'

For three decades, any person dispatched to interview Tom Waits has found they rarely get a straight answer. During the 1980s, after he met his wife and they began their family, which now numbers three children, he understandably became a much more closed person, protecting his family's privacy as best he could. But it's not just his family he protects. Interviews with Waits are always highly entertaining. He is a fabulous conversationalist and a reporter would never leave a Tom Waits interview short of copy. But after reading interviews, one is struck by the fact that you still know very little about the man. He openly 'plays' with the interviewer, retreating behind sharp-witted babble, tossing out smoke screens, red herrings and, amongst these, sudden confessions. As an artist working in public view, he is certainly not obliged to disclose anything about his private self, yet like most people, some days he says too much and on others he sends his questioners through the looking glass to chase the rabbit. Like the fairytale creature Rumpelstiltskin, he keeps us guessing his secret name.

Kathleen Brennan does not appear in public with Waits when promoting their collaborative work. He maintains a discreet front for her, inventing a past as a circus performer, elevator operator and as mambo singer Yma Sumac's hairdresser, amongst other things. But he also maintains a very straightforward respect for her abilities to help him get beyond himself, to ease him out of worn melodic and textural pathways. In an exchange with Elvis Costello transcribed in *Option* magazine in 1989, Waits mentioned that he and his wife see a different spectrum. Using colour as a metaphor and, apparently also literally, he noted that he will be seeing red and yellow, quite clearly differentiated, whereupon Brennan will point out that he's 'created sludge', shades of grubby brown. Their working together creates an interesting conflict, especially for a writer like Waits, who had been a one-man operation for quite some time.

They are clearly very attuned to each other creatively. Since they met, Waits' albums have featured very sincere, very simple love songs written for Kathleen, starting with the lovely 'Johnsburg, Illinois' on *Swordfishtrombones*. They have now been married for twenty years. When measuring a rock 'n' roll marriage, you have to count time like dog years, so that would be around 140 years of regular matrimony. Waits has referred to her as a lapsed Catholic who still retains a deep sense of spiritual questioning and who incorporates a lot of biblical imagery in her work. Francis Thumm, Waits' musical collaborator on the pivotal *Swordfishtrombones,* claims that Waits' life can be divided into two, before and after Kathleen. More than anyone, she seems to have given him the support to turn within and explore some more personal imagery.

'I thought I was a millionaire, and it turned out that I had, like, twenty bucks.' Waits speaks of the 'bumpy ride' the newly-weds experienced, as Brennan encouraged Waits to go ahead and produce his own album despite Waits' tentative business situation after his split from Herb Cohen. At the prompting of his wife, he began to take stock of his broad-ranging musical preferences and added some new ones; 'She's a great DJ and she started playing a lot of records for me.' From this beginning,

Waits found he was able to take a song from the writing stage to finished product without having to have an outside producer in to guide or validate it. 'The seminal idea for *Swordfishtrombones* really came from Kathleen.' With the assistance of engineer Biff Dawes, they put together a four-song demo, but Joe Smith, Waits' label boss, wasn't overwhelmed by the new sound. 'At that point I was kind of dropped from the label.' Fortunately for the record-buying public, Island Records' Chris Blackwell was very interested.

In the Spring of 1981, Waits set out to tour Europe. This time Kathleen came along and they finally took their honeymoon in Ireland, which sounds a lot more romantic than Waits' summary of their wedding: he claims they found a marriage chapel in the phone book, right next to the 'Massage' section. In September of that year, he finished his work on *One From The Heart*, which went on to receive an Oscar nomination in 1982 for Best Original Film Score. The film itself was not so well received. This album was Bones Howe's last work with Waits and featured country favourite Crystal Gayle duetting with Waits and singing a couple of his songs solo.

It was around this time that Bruce Springsteen recorded his version of 'Jersey Girl' from *Heartattack,* and the two actually performed the song together when Springsteen played in Los Angeles in August of that year. In the meantime, Waits and Brennan had been at work on *Swordfishtrombones*. It was recorded with Biff Dawes, a veteran engineer who had worked on Bob Dylan's *Street Legal* in 1978 and who here began a long association with Waits. They booked into Sunset Sound studios in August 1982, but they soon found that Elektra would not be willing to accommodate this new musical vision. Waits found Island Records' Chris Blackwell much more willing to support his new direction and Waits signed to the label in 1983. Waits also parted company with his last link to his former life, Herb Cohen. The management company noted on the 'Swordfishtrombones' sleeve was now the Rothberg/Gerber company. The publishing credits also reflected the change. Cohen's Fifth Floor Music ceased to own Waits' songs after *One From The Heart*, Waits' work being published by Jalma Music from then on. The Waits family briefly moved to New York, where he made the acquaintance of more like-minded souls such as new-wave jazz artist and actor John Lurie of the Lounge Lizards, and the film-maker Jim Jarmusch. He, Lurie, and Lurie's brother Evan shared a workroom in Greenwich village where Waits would go to write late into the night, and then return home, a similar approach to the one he took at Zoetrope, except that this time there were fewer memos. *Swordfishtrombones* was finally released in September 1983 and Waits dedicated the album to his wife, who, he says, co-produced the collection: 'she was the spark and the feed.' Their first child was born in that same year.

Although he may have not have been completely serious, Waits once confessed: 'I have an auditory processing problem that is probably at the centre of my work.' Despite the story he told about his night-time hyper-sensitivity to sound as a teenager, Waits' musical sense in the albums leading up to *Swordfishtrombones* shows a musician and singer with a keen ear for such conventions as pitch and accompaniment. Ironically, the last of the albums of his 'early' career, *One From The Heart*, is also Waits' most musically conservative – and reveals he can sing very well when he wants to. However, the way he relates to the texture of sound is a different matter. Once he climbed over the wall in 1982 and made *Swordfishtrombones*, he didn't stop.

Waits' sense of songs and the rooms in which they are recorded is engagingly whimsical. He seems to believe that the conception of a song is a mystery often out of the control of the apparent creator. When working with Rolling Stone guitar hero Keith Richards on *Rain Dogs* and *Bone Machine*, he observed that Richards and he wrote in a similar fashion: 'you kind of circle [the song], and you sneak up on it.' Waits has an affection and respect for songs, which in his eyes are no longer abstract things, but self-contained individuals with little souls. He says 'Songs ... some of them are little paramedics. Or maybe some will be killers. Some of them will die on the windshield. And some of them will never leave home.' This is a variation of the empathy he has expressed for old instruments and mechanisms that seem to be animated by their own breath. The quavering dignity of steam whistles, fairground organs and gasping old accordions is honoured and upheld by Waits from *Swordfishtrombones* onward. His great sympathy for outcasts and freaks is illuminated by his comment, 'I guess most entertainers are, on a certain level, part of the freakshow. And most of them have some kind of wounding early on.' This early damage, he said, can send them on an odyssey that can end with them 'kneeling by a jukebox, praying to Ray Charles'.

Swordfishtrombones featured Greg Cohen and Larry Taylor, as well as Francis Thumm. Thumm, as will be discussed later, had a long-standing familiarity with the use of unorthodox instrumentation, having worked with the visionary instrument maker and musician Harry Partch. Waits describes Thumm, whom he has known for thirty years, as coming from a regimented background, having the discipline that Waits says he lacks. He also jests that Thumm's appreciative familiarity with Ballantine's whisky has lead him into all sorts of trouble, making him sound like an avant-garde Chuck E Weiss (Thumm is credited on *Bone Machine* as the 'musical security guard'.) Of the new songs, Waits says he tried to allow the music to take on the features of each track's characters. Before, he said, although there were unique voices, it was as if all the people wore the same clothes.

As usual, autumn was taken up by promotional tours for the album, which was rapturously received by the critics and recognized as the watershed that it was. Waits was now taking a little more time between album releases. The next year, he was contacted by producer Hal Willner, who was putting together a Kurt Weill celebration album, to be called *Lost In The Stars*. Willner tended to work with a very Waitsian cast of artists, the jazz eclectics and the nouveau roots crowd. The people he gathered for this project, and a later Disney song tribute, which also included Waits, were drawn from this talent pool: John Zorn, Stan Ridgway, Van Dyke Parks, Ken Nordine, Yma Sumac and Buster Poindexter (former New York Doll David Johansen). This time, Waits did a version of 'What Keeps Mankind Alive?' from *The Threepenny Opera*. Waits has praised Willner's way of working as 'a producer who lets things happen and knows when to back off'. Willner introduced him to the former 1960s pop icon, Marianne Faithfull, with whom Willner had recorded 'Ballad Of The Soldiers Wife' for *Lost...* Her quivering, dewy, neo-folk act was by now a distant memory, as was the heroin addiction she had picked up during her notorious youth in the company of the Rolling Stones. In 1979 Faithfull released the highly regarded album *Broken English*, a harsh, world-weary, post-rock cabaret assault. Her voice was a sexy ruin, and a fine vehicle for a Tom Waits song, it was agreed by all. There had been some discussion of Waits writing a full-length album for Faithfull. As it was, he (together with Brennan) composed 'Strange Weather', which was released on the album of the same name in 1987. Waits himself did not record it for release until 1988, when it appeared on the live album *Big Time*.

The second album of the trilogy, recorded in New York, was released at the end of September 1985. *Rain Dogs* draws heavily on Waits' 1980s image bank of nightmare sailors, hurdy-gurdys and nineteenth-century Americana, but also has some straightforward and lovely classics. It features the song Rod Stewart took to number three in 1989, 'Downtown Train', 'Time' and 'Hang Down Your Head', a beautiful mid-tempo creation co-written with Brennan. One of the best performances comes in the sinisterly syncopated Latin tilt-a-whirl of 'Jockey Full Of Bourbon'. Guitarist and sometime Lounge Lizard Marc Ribot makes his Waits debut on this album and 'Jockey' wonderfully documents his ability to co-opt genres, in this case the Mexican Western, and distil them into something simple and precise. Also featured on the album is Keith Richards, who contributes to 'Big Black Mariah' and 'Union Square'. Richards must have enjoyed himself, for he returned in 1992 to co-write 'That Feel' for *Bone Machine*. 'He stands... in the middle of the room and does those Chuck Berry splits' confirmed Waits, describing recording with the near-mythical Richards.

Rain Dogs was a worldwide success and in the autumn of 1985 Waits took the show on the road. Owing to a misunderstanding with Dutch customs, Waits was to remove the Netherlands from his touring itinerary for a few years. It would seem he was unfortunate enough to go through Amsterdam's Schiphol Airport, at a time when the customs agency was toughening up its anti-drug act. Waits has told several variations on the story, all with a common theme, most notably to Dutch writer, Bert van de Kamp, who was contrite enough to apologize for the entire nation in 1988. Waits was detained for between twelve and thirty-eight hours, depending on which version he tells. The reason remains unknown and no charges were brought against him. He suggested that wearing a brassiere outside his overcoat and carrying cash was reason enough, but that's probably not entirely true on any level. He claims to have arranged to meet with his cellmates, an assortment of characters from Senegal, Indonesia and Vietnam (and the obligatory three hookers from Portugal), on a yearly basis. Yet again, Waits seemed to have painted himself into one of his songs. The Dutch, bless them all, must have been truly penitent, for seven years later they bought *The Black Rider* in such quantities that it stayed in their Top 40 for six whole weeks. At the end of that year, *Rolling Stone* voted Waits 'Songwriter of the Year.'

This was the decade that Waits consolidated the theatrical element in both his work and his public persona. He had a multitude of smallish roles and a couple of major appearances in movies, and then moved on to stage plays. His film roles included *The Stone Boy* and *The Cotton Club*, both in 1982, and *Rumblefish* and *The Outsiders* in 1983. In 1985, Jim Jarmusch cast him in his first major role, alongside John Lurie and Robert Benigni, in *Down By Law*. 'I wrote that movie with Tom and John in mind,' said Jarmusch later.

In 1987, he began filming his role as Rudy in *Ironweed*, alongside Meryl Streep and Jack Nicholson. Here, he said, he learned a great deal about putting together a narrative and characters. He took this experience into *Frank's Wild Years*. Between 1986 and 1990, Waits the actor also showed up in *Candy Mountain, Cold Feet, Bearskin, The Two Jakes* and appeared as the voice of a radio DJ in another Jarmusch favourite, *Mystery Train*.

Of his acting career, Waits has noted that he's often more interested in smaller parts in movies. Film writer Christopher

Connely has identified a couple of reasons for Waits' continued success on screen, apart from his obvious charisma. Unlike other musicians crossing over, such as Sting or Madonna, he remains a character actor which allows him more range. He is also a little more obscure and 'not used up as a cultural icon'. This shields him from the hyper-critical attention directed at stars such as Madonna.

After the change of style unveiled in *Swordfishtrombones*, Waits' next landmark opus was the stage play and musical *Frank's Wild Years*, written with Brennan and described by her as an *Operachi Romantico*, which is a lovely way of avoiding the unspeakable – and inappropriate – rock opera tag. The play was staged by Chicago's prestigious Steppenwolf Theater company, at the Briar Street Theater, where it had a three-month run. It was here that Waits made his live theatre debut. 'A play takes a lot of energy – emotionally, financially. And the other thing is that it only lives when you're in it. But Steppenwolf was the right way to go.'

Waits described the play as a cross between a Jacqueline Susann novel and the Bible. Robert Wilson, who later worked on *Black Rider*, had been the first person Waits had thought of, but Wilson didn't know how to take Waits' idea for a play. Frank is a has-been accordion player and the play begins with him on a park bench. We have previously met Frank in the song 'Frank's Wild Years' from *Swordfishtrombones*, where we get the back story. When asked by *Spin* magazine's Glenn O' Brien what he had to learn in order to take to the stage as an actor, Waits responded, 'I just have to learn honest, truthful behaviour, that's all.' The play was a major collaboration for Waits and Brennan. In the *Spin* interview, Waits made a very rare Groucho Marx-style marriage joke: when asked if they worked together, or if they sent stuff back and forth, Waits responded,

'We sent stuff back and forth. Like dishes, books, frying pans, vases.'

Frank's Wild Years was recorded in Los Angeles and Chicago, and featured the usual suspects: Greg Cohen, Marc Ribot, Larry Taylor, Francis Thumm and a guest appearance from Los Lobos' David Hidalgo. He took the album on tour in the autumn of 1987. In 1989, Waits took on another theatrical challenge, this time his first full-length, live theatre appearance in a play written by someone else. He showed up alongside Bud Cort and Carol Kane in Thomas Babe's *Demon Wine*. The play was staged by the Los Angeles Theater Company.

By now, Waits had certainly expanded the public's perception of his work, and he returned to music by putting together a video of mostly concert footage and an accompanying album. *Big Time* was recorded live in San Francisco, Dublin, Stockholm, Berlin and Los Angeles, with the exception of the stately 'Falling Down', a studio recording. He was accompanied by Michael Blair on drums and percussion, Ralph Carney on brass and woodwind, Greg Cohen, bass, Marc Ribot, guitar, and Willie Schwarz on organ, sitar and accordion. All the songs featured were from the *Swordfishtrombones* era onward, with only two, 'Ruby's Arms' and 'Red Shoes' from the Elektra Asylum era.

The next decade was to see the merging of the two sides of Waits, the melancholy American era and the more unruly European element. He recorded two albums that were to appeal to a new generation of listeners, not by picking up on new trends, but by simply having remained himself and waited for musical modes to catch up with him. Unfortunately, he also spent a good part of the decade wrapped up in legal complications.

In September and October 1988, around 250 radio stations aired commercials for Frito-Lay snack products, voiced by a

Waits soundalike singing a variation on 'Step Right Up'. In November he sued the company and was ultimately awarded damages totalling $2.5 million.

In the early 1990s, he and Herb Cohen were to be enmeshed in a complex series of claims and counterclaims over Waits' songs and recordings between the years of 1972 and 1982. The first problem arose when Cohen's Third Story Music label decided to issue *The Early Years* demo tapes for commercial sale. Although Waits tried to prevent the release, the songs came out on the Manifesto label in 1991.

There was more friction between Herb Cohen and Waits when they exchanged suits in 1993 over several Waits songs ('Heartattack And Vine', 'Ruby's Arms' and some music from *One From The Heart*) which Cohen wished to licence to some French, British and Argentine companies for use in their commercials. Waits has always gone to great lengths to avoid being considered a commercial commodity and to protect the artistic integrity of his work. Waits prevailed in these law suits, although his request for damages for lost income was not successful. Judge Harvey A Schneider wrote in one decision, 'A songwriter... has a legitimate concern that his compositions may be denigrated by their use in commercials.' However, the same judge was not convinced that the songs would be rendered commercially valueless thereafter. Ironically, this exchange took place just before the extreme commercialization of Top 40 music, at a time when selling songs to commercials was viewed with a great deal of disdain by the older generation of artists. A new breed of pop musician has since emerged, one which is only too happy to see their songs play on a commercial at the same time as they are released to radio.

Since then, there have been two Tom Waits tribute albums released by Evan Cohen's Manifesto Records. The first in 1995,

Step Right Up and the latest, in 2000, *New Coat Of Paint*. A broad range of artists, from 10,000 Maniacs to Lydia Lunch, are featured, covering Waits' songs from 1972–1982. *Step Right Up* was voted best tribute album of 1995 by *Pulse* magazine.

The album *Bone Machine* brought Waits to the attention of a younger audience. The San Francisco trio Primus were featured on the album (Waits had appeared on their *Sailing The Seas Of Cheese* singing 'Tommy The Cat' in 1991). They popped up again on *Mule Variations* and then asked Waits to produce a track on their 1999 multi-collaborative album, *AntiPop*. He was a little wary of asserting himself as a producer until they told him the title, 'Coattails Of A Dead Man', whereupon he couldn't get into the studio fast enough. *Bone Machine* features a Chamberlain Music Master, an ancient precursor to the sampler. It is organ-like in appearance and contains around seventy sounds and voices, carried in little tape loops. Waits has professed himself touched by the sounds made by inanimate things. The weary old Chamberlain was no exception. Waits said he discovered it in Westwood where some surfers were making fun of it. He rescued the old trouper: 'I saw it and said, "I'll take you home now, dear."' Waits had used it once before, on *Frank's Wild Years*. Waits unveiled his 'Prince voice' on this collection, a splendid wobbling falsetto, lisping over the boxy drums. The album was awarded a Grammy for Best Alternative Rock Performance in 1992.

In 1992, the soundtrack for *Night On Earth* was released, another Brennan/Waits cooperation. The album gave Waits another opportunity to rescue more lost sounds from yesteryear. He has expressed admiration for folk song collector and sound archivist Alan Lomax's efforts to keep the sounds of America alive, recording not just singers in the field, but also the sounds of old cash registers. Waits speaks of a growing obsession with train whistles, citing an acquaintance who has pitched four octaves of train whistles that enabled Waits to play the 'train whistle organ'.

The album *Black Rider* was released in 1993, using some of the original recordings of a production which was conceived and first performed in Hamburg over the period 1989 to 1990. Later recordings were made in the USA using a similar approach. In May of 1989, Waits went to Hamburg, Germany, to begin work on the musical play of the album. He was to work with playwright Robert Wilson, and was to also engage the services of literary legend William S Burroughs. The play was premiered in March of the following year at the Thalia Theater in Hamburg. Waits was to spend a great deal of time collaborating with musician Greg Cohen, with whom he had worked on several albums. Waits described him as 'an arranger and stamp collector', and goes into more detail in the sleeve notes on *The Black Rider* CD, describing him as a multi-instrumentalist and fearless collaborator, unfazed by the long hours, cold coffee and lack of a place to lie down. Robert Wilson, whose production *Einstein On The Beach* had first drawn Waits to his work, is noted as 'an inventor on a journey of discovery into the deepest parts of the forest of the mind... '

The album is surprisingly accessible, although the introductory track may cause more faint-hearted listeners to drop their knitting, as the feverish bellowing of a crazed carnival master cuts in. It's a part folk-song, part Tom Waits album, with lots of careening Kurt Weill orchestration and stomping boots. William Burroughs not only contributes lyrically, but also sings a little. Waits compares him first to a 'metal desk', then, less obscurely, to a still. 'Everything that comes out of him is whisky.' He also observed of Burroughs, 'He had a strongly developed sense of irony, and I guess that's really at the heart of the American experience.' Waits has been deeply impressed by the work Burroughs had done with Hal Willner, the man behind the *Lost In The Stars* Weill tribute. It's not that surprising to learn that when Waits released *Swordfishtrombones*, he had really not listened to Weill's work at all – the style came naturally to him. When people began to compare his new style to the German Expressionist, Waits thought, 'I better go find out who this guy is.' He was to find that he heard a lot of anger in Weill's songs.

The songs were recorded 'very crudely' in Hamburg, says Waits. 'I like to… scratch it up… go further into that world of texture.' He speaks of working at unusually high speeds with players who have been trained classically, who, in doing this, got to explore more spontaneous approaches to music. Waits is constantly checking himself. He forces himself to use unfamiliar instruments, so he doesn't end up playing in the comfort zone. Hands at the piano, he says, are like dogs. They go to the places they know. Robert Wilson and Waits have begun work on another collaboration, a production of the Georg Büchner drama *Woyzeck*, which was due to premier in November 2000 in Denmark as part of the Culture Bridge 2000 Celebration, to commemorate the new bridge linking Denmark with Sweden.

The musical play Waits had worked on with Paul Schmidt and Kathleen Brennan, *Alice*, opened in in New York City in late 1995. This was a story inspired by the young girl, Alice Liddell, who was the muse of the rather sinister Lewis Carroll. A few months later, Waits made a rare live appearance at the Paramount Theater in Oakland. It was a benefit for his friend Don Hyde who had been accused of illegal drug trading. Although Hyde's defence was successful, a second benefit was necessary to cover the additional legal bills. It took yet another benefit to lure Waits out of his northern California seclusion. The Not In Our Name concert, also featuring Ani Di Franco, Eddie Vedder and Lyle Lovett, took place in Los Angeles in March 1998 and sought to raise money for families of murder victims and for those whose relatives had suffered the death penalty.

In September 1999, record buyers were offered a rare treat. Ryko released an album by Jack Kerouac, recorded sometime in the 1950s, reading from his own work. A sparkling throng of new musicians gathered in 1999 to play the musical accompaniment. Primus and Waits were amongst them and they finish the album with a version of 'On The Road'. But probably the most significant tribute album to feature Waits was the Kinky Friedman album released in late 1998, on which Waits covered his 'Highway Cafe'. Obviously he must have forgiven Friedman for invading the stage in New Orleans, way back in 1975. Also contributing to the collection was Tom's old buddy Chuck E Weiss.

On the last day of March 1998, Waits told listeners to Chris Douridas' show on KCRW in Los Angeles that he would be leaving Island Records, but would be starting work on a new album and true to his word, he went into Prairie Sun Studios in early summer to start work on the glorious *Mule Variations*. In a rather startling move, in mid-June, he announced that he had struck a one-album deal with the independent label Epitaph, whose speciality was various kinds of grinding, unforgiving nouvelle punk. Waits decided he would feel quite at home there, and was especially impressed that the label went to the support of one of their acts who were seeking to stop their record being played on the radio. Waits has a horror of his work being perceived as a commodity, and here was a label which would respect his integrity. He went on to reward their kind understanding by selling bucketloads of *Mule Variations*.

The title, he said, was inspired to some degree by Robert Johnson, the man popularly referred to as 'The Father of the Blues'. Johnson's father would urge his son to 'get behind the mule', meaning stop sitting around playing that guitar and make something of your life. Waits mused that many a time he himself had risen too late to get behind the mule. The mule had already gone, or, he had to get behind the man who was first behind the mule. However, Waits has also mentioned that his wife has accused him of stubborn, mule-like behaviour, so there's probably a little of that there as well. The album is Waits' move to 'get back to the land'. Robert Johnson, he said, picking on the hapless bluesman again, started writing about automobiles and, thereafter, no one wrote about animals any more.

The album was recorded in a converted chicken shack with Waits' favourite players and several newer San Francisco Bay Area musicians. Waits claims that if you trust the environment, the outdoors with its unpredictable chickens and aeroplanes, it will cooperate by intruding in perfect time. The album blends grunge, old blues field hollers and neo-Springsteenisms. The songs are sometimes a little more sentimental than usual, but never cloying. Waits suggests he might be a little more at peace with himself, less afraid of what people might say, a little more willing to be vulnerable. But having admitted to that, he adds that he may have gone too far in the direction of the heart: 'Tomorrow, I may write nothing but astronaut music for ten years.'

A visit to Epitaph's delightful website reveals that the fans either love or hate the album (which actually seems to be the reaction to all Epitaph releases, but that's not the point). Some youngsters are horrified, 'What the F***'s this??!!!' they cry in capital letters, unable to cope with Waits' voice, as they stumble back to the comfort of their Choking Victim album where they are soothed by the sounds of the band's satano-political ska/punk musings.

Tom Waits took the 1999–2000 'Get Behind The Mule' tour across North America and Europe, stopping off in Austin, Texas for an appearance at the South By Southwest annual gathering of music-business heavyweights. He was nominated for two Grammys, one for Best Male Rock Vocal Performance (for the single 'Hold On') and the other (for which he actually received the Grammy) for best Contemporary Folk Album. The record went on to sell nearly a million copies worldwide, which is a significant achievement for an independent label, just in terms of supplying the demand. A second album with Epitaph has been rumoured but not confirmed. Waits' presence laid a path for Merle Haggard to follow, for it seems that the craggy and very particular country star is all set to follow Waits to Epitaph. Tom Waits had not been on the road for six years and was unsure of who his audience were, or even if he still had one. Obviously he did still have one, but it was sweet of him to worry about it. He found himself set to play on a bill with Fishbone, and was concerned that the two separate audiences, his and theirs, would not appreciate both acts. But his fretting was unfounded and he found the energy of the Fishbone fans to be most inspiring. He maintains a self-searching approach, wanting to be sure that he is not touring just to have his ego petted. Waits has said on more than one occasion that he is afraid to find himself in the situation where he has been trying for a long time to get attention, tapping the world on the shoulder. Afraid that when the world finally turns around and asks what he has to say, that he will have completely forgotten what it was. This is a rare conscientiousness in an artist who has been successful for as long as Waits has. It also seems rather unlikely, given that Waits seem to have an answer for everything. When asked by a reporter from MTV why it took him six whole years to go back into the studio to make an album, Waits replied, 'I was stuck in traffic'. Which is pretty much where he came in.

TWO

THE MUSIC

Waits' full-length original albums are considered first. There are no chart placings noted – noting chart positions on a Tom Waits discography is like putting Barbie clothes on a bulldog. He's just not that kind of artist, despite the fact that he sells many thousands of records and sells out live venues within hours. Included in the first part are the two albums of 1971 demo recordings. These are not true original releases but are significant enough to cast light on the artist's musical development.

Closing Time

```
Released:  1973
   Label:  Asylum/Elektra
Producer:  Jerry Yester
Engineer:  Richie Moore
Recorded:  Sunset Sound, Hollywood, 1973
```

Waits was twenty-four when he recorded this first full-length album, and it is something of an oddity in the Waits Hall of Fame. It's a very sincere man-at-his-piano piece, with rhymes in all the proper places, but there are shadowy complexities lurking in there and as a collection it lies down gently and waits for your attention. Old-fashioned strings and muted trumpets wander tentatively through, Waits' voice is a little gruff, a little shaky but has a deep burnish and a powerful presence.

Ol' 55

The up-down, up-down piano accompaniment seems to be going way too slow, but once Waits put the vocal on board, he can carry the stately pace with ease. A classic trust-only-your-car song with an red-blooded country-rock harmony on the chorus. This is the song The Eagles made into something more aerodynamic. Waits counts the song in, which you have to love. Whatever happened to counting?

I Hope That I Don't Fall In Love With You

A sweet little piece of irony, the guy in the bar drinking his way to falling in love with a stranger who leaves before he can speak to her. Pretty picking, pretty melody, pretty song.

Virginia Avenue

An old-fashioned tumbling blues scale sets the scene for a mannered, after-hours jazz strut. Waits gets to escape the honest-self voice and move towards phrasing that is a little looser and dirty.

Old Shoes (& Picture Postcards)

A slow-stepping, righteous southern rock waltz. Travis Tritt carries the banner for songs like this these days. This and 'Ol' 55' show that as both a songwriter and a singer, Waits could have gone for a career that would have made him patron saint of Austin, Texas.

Midnight Lullaby

Brooding, melancholic Ray Charles-isms reveal unexpected vocal sophistication. Waits had obviously studied Mom and Dad's record collection in detail.

Martha

Such a sad song for a young man to be singing. Waits seems to age four decades to portray a gravelly old boy calling up his ex of forty years ago, for old times' sake. There is something about his longing for the innocence of a faded but troubled youth that suggests that this person had been waiting all his life to be old enough to mis-remember what life wasn't like. An agonizing, beautiful, beaten-down Harry Chapin kind of song.

Rosie

A soundly constructed post-folk song, looks good whichever way you hold it.

Lonely

A lovely sun-dappled progression up a Randy Newman scale, the single notes pooling in bright, white spaces. The simple elegance is about as far away from *Small Change* as one could get, but the idea of a theme-with-vocal, as opposed to a song, does lay the founda-tions for his later excursions into film and theatre.

Ice Cream Man

A jaunty, happy finger-snapper, the type that should get Harry Connick Jnr fans dancing in the aisles. The fiendishly real ice cream van chimes at the end will always disappoint the kids, so be careful or have a well-stocked freezer.

Little Trip To Heaven (On The Wings Of Your Love)

A truly romantic Hollywood smoochathon, rendered with just the right mellow bluesy timbre. A cinematic, soft-focus lullaby that leans more towards Louis Armstrong than Perry Como.

Grapefruit Moon

A very upright composition, crammed with all the quiet virtues and starry-eyed decency that one expects from musicals such as *Annie*. Drama teachers across the world should be setting this as an end-of-term concert piece for nine-year-olds. Not that there's anything wrong with that.

Closing Time

More melancholy, empty rooms lit with shafts of bittersweet Californian sunlight. An easygoing piano and muted trumpet instrumental with some shadowy strings. A very 1970s contemporary feel, a mode that was to evaporate completely with the next album.

Heart Of Saturday Night

Released: 1974
Label: Asylum/Elektra
Producer: Bones Howe
Engineers: Bones Howe, Geoff Howe
Recorded: Wally Heider Recording, Hollywood, 1974

Having felt his debut album veered too much towards folk and violins, Waits sought the assistance of LA jazz veteran producer, Bones Howe. In the course of one year, Waits had matured significantly, spouting his first recorded song-poems with a weathered authority. The orchestral arrangements of Mike Melvoin give the album a classic sophistication. Ironically, the strings are much more noticeable than on Closing Time *but they serve to make a clear statement about where Waits' roots lie.*

New Coat Of Paint

A very mature New Orleans jazz piano sashay.

San Diego Serenade

Some of the traditional songwriter habits remain, you can tell because Tom still both uses the word 'melody' in a song and pronounces it mel-oh-dcc.

Semi Suite

'Truck drivin' man stoppin' when he can'. An easy slide through some late-night blue-collar imagery.

Shiver Me Timbers

A genuine classic, the set of poetic images is more than a narrative of signifiers: 'the clouds are like headlines/on a new front page sky'.

Diamonds On My Windshield

A zig-zagging walking bass sets the pace for a mannered driver-and-hitchhiker jazz poem.

(Looking For) The Heart Of Saturday Night

Another beauty, a broken ode to empty cruising and the strange, unfounded yearnings that fuel it. A faultlessly arranged backing, discreet country-jazz bass, a song that cries out for a verse to be sung by Willie Nelson.

Fumblin' With The Blues

Waits takes on the persona of a swinger twice his age and the band takes up his cause with gusto. A very convincing performance, almost verging on caricature. It's the sort of song you can imagine being given to a womanizing animated reptile in a Disney cartoon. Probably one the songs that inspired Muppets creator Jim Henson to model Rowlf the piano-playing dog in Waits' image.

Please Call Me, Baby

'If I exorcise my devils, my angels may leave too'. An affectionate don't-sleep-in-the-subway pleader, almost conversational crooning over a sympathetic orchestra.

Depot, Depot

Woozy blues word associations do their best to justify the brilliant title. An astoundingly eloquent trumpet solo squawks over super-hip layered horns, saying just enough and no more.

Drunk On The Moon

More 1940s rainy night discreet orchestrations over some highly stylized vocal phrasing.

The Ghosts Of Saturday Night (After Hours At Napoleone's Pizza House)

This is where the Lounge Waits of the mid-1970s steps out, fully formed, muttering, crooning, drawling, writing about waitresses and batting around off-the-wall metaphors and similes. Here, his writer's voice is strangely akin to that of *Owl And The Pussycat* nonsense poet Edward Lear.

Nighthawks at the Diner

Released: 1975
Label: Elektra/Asylum
Producer: Bones Howe
Engineer: Bones Howe
Recorded: The Record Plant Wally Heider Recording,
Hollywood, July 30 & 31, 1975

A live album of new material, recorded in front of an invited studio audience. The intricate witticisms and humour wear well over the duration of just one album, but any more records like this would be verging on the indulgent. Waits shows himself to be genial, modest, whimsical, poetically vulgar and an outstanding writer. A classic jazz quartet backs him, piano swelling up in big square crescendos when Waits reaches a lyrical punch-line. His voice is very different, ragged, emphysemic, the voice of a much older man. And, good heavens, that laugh… a dorky chortle that would put Beavis and Butthead to shame.

Emotional Weather Report
Preceded by a quip about the crack of dawn that could be quite unsavoury, but Tom gets away with it. This weather report is an elaborately droll rap: 'tornado watches issued… for… the areas including the western region of my mental health'.

On A Foggy Night
Shades of Billie Holiday here, free-flowing moody Raymond Chandler-isms. Tres cool.

Eggs & Sausage (In A Cadillac With Susan Michelson)

Songs that talk about food (savoury, not sweet – big difference) tread a fine line. The mere mention in just one song of home cooking, or even ordering off a diner menu, can quickly de-eroticize an artist's entire back catalogue. There are exceptions, people who can sing about it and stay fly; wheezing Cajuns and Hank Williams, Bessie Smith, kitchen sink drab realists like Squeeze... and Tom Waits. This list is not very big.

Better Off Without A Wife

'She's been married so many times she's got rice marks all over her face', quips Waits in his marriage monologue. A shuffling, cuddly hangdog of a song.

Nighthawk Postcards

Very beat, far-ranging urban poetry, musing on salesmanship and favourite records, 'decent factory air and AM–FM dreams' and coming back to low-rent reality, a constant effort to meet 'one low monthly payment through the nose'. Waits' sense of drama is understated and immaculate, and some of his language preposterous, where a 'buttery cueball moon' rolls across an 'obsidian sky', but that's kind of what the album is here for, to claim some rugged literary hinterland to act as distant scenery for his later work.

Warm Beer And Cold Women

Bending mournful end notes, a pitiful paean to alienation and booze at the last chance saloon.

Putnam County

Leaving behind the bars and shoddy city neon, it's off to small-town America, the real America. The radio 'spits out Charlie Rich' as Waits swoops over the pre-dawn streets of the 'dark, warm, narcotic

American night', observing the inevitable Everyday, and then zooms into a home for a close up of the 'porcelain poodles and glass swans' (cheers of recognition from the audience), followed by 'the toilet's runnin', uh Christ, shake the handle,' (louder cheers of recognition). A poetic jewel. A quiet piano plays a slow burn motif and the sax buzzes softly so as not to wake the sleepers of Putnam County.

Spare Parts I (A Nocturnal Emission)

Written with Chuck E Weiss, a snappy, hip soft-shoe back to the city: 'the stew bums showed up just like bounced checks'. Pete Christlieb's sax makes some arch moves in the right direction. Some scuttling, twisting delivery and credible scat singing, the kind that sounds like the singer's tongue has been stapled to his bottom front teeth.

Nobody

A disarmingly simple, old-fashioned song, more shades of Louis Armstrong, a one-too-many slow dance for the solitary.

Big Joe And Phantom 309

A song written by Tommy Faile and once performed by country and western king, Red Sovine. Waits' sense of rhythm sometimes gets in the way of the narrative: you can hear him almost get distracted by the pleasing flow of a sentence, so he retraces his steps and repeats it. A telling choice of song to cover, country and western having been the stronghold of the American musical storytellers. Sovine was renowned for spinning morbid tales that verged on Victorian melodrama. Waits retells this story with no trace of irony.

Small Change

Released: 1976
Label: Elektra/Asylum
Producer: Bones Howe
Engineers: Bones Howe, Geoff Howe and Bills Broms
Recorded: Wally Heider Recording, Hollywood,
July 15, 19, 20, 21, 29, 1976

Everything suddenly sounds much more personal, Waits'
tales of the warm, narcotic American night now have a
heart-rending, first-person sense about them. The scat-
singing wise-cracker from Nighthawks *has begun to feel*
the damage. From now on, every word Waits sings
seems to require his every last effort and seems to
cause bloody carnage in his throat. Jerry Yester returns to
add some string arrangements.

Tom Traubert's Blues (Four Sheets To The Wind In Copenhagen)

'Wasted and wounded, it ain't what the moon did', begins Waits
with a quiet howl. What on earth happened to this poor man?
Famous for its incorporation of the 'Waltzing Matilda' chorus, Tom
used to like to close his shows with this.

Step Right Up

A quick-tripping shuffle as Waits sells off the bargain goods, rattling
off the cheap infomercial clichés and poetry of bottom-line commerce. Jim Hughart's insistent walking, looping bass will delight,
impress and ultimately drive you bonkers.

Jitterbug Boy (Sharing A Curbstone With Chuck E Weiss, Robert Marchese, Paul Body And The Mug And Artie)

A cartoon Tom holds up a lamppost and reminisces on his modern American heritage, a wonderfully complete little dramatic piece. You can bet Rowlf the dog was taking notes.

I Wish I Was In New Orleans (In The Ninth Ward)

A song that could have been written in 1875, except it mentions ol' Chuck E Weiss. One of those instant classic Waits songs that you swear you have heard before. For a man who professes to hate musical theatre, he has written some ageless compositions that beg for a play to tie them all together.

The Piano Has Been Drinking (Not Me)(An Evening With Pete King)

Another classic, a tragi-comic drunkard's lament, except this piano player is way too lucid: 'the owner is a mental midget with the IQ of a fencepost'. He must have loved to slip that line in on the club nights that weren't going too well.

Invitation To The Blues

A midnight-blue, Runyonesque pastiche, except the regret is real, taking form as the singer's melancholic yearning for the waitress of the moment: 'but you can't take your eyes off her/Get another cup of java'. Bus stations, diners and secondhand suitcases, those sorrowful frames of the human condition.

Pasties And A G-String (At The Two O'Clock Club)

Slim Gaillard-style appreciation of striptease artists. Addictive.

Bad Liver And A Broken Heart (In Lowell)

Begins by hinting at 'As Time Goes By' before turning into a few minutes of hard-growled listening.

The One That Got Away

A glorious light piece of smart-talking jazz poetry, with Lew Tabackin's sax squalling in pleasing, twisting little strokes. 'Don't know how to spell her name but she's the one that got away.'

Small Change (Got Rained On With His Own .38)

Again, Tabackin's sax meanders darkly and discreetly for this beat elegy for a young gangster shot dead with his own gun. Waits declaims with the authority of a professional mourner.

I Can't Wait To Get Off Work (And See My Baby On Montgomery Avenue)

Nobody dies, nobody's trying to escape their lives. An adorable, romantic drudge anthem: guy working late into the night, cleaning up, dreaming of baby as the bossman nags, 'Do this, don't do that. Tom! Don't do that'. The song maybe suffers from its proximity to the pain and the morbid ache of the rest of the album, but it's a nice way to end.

Foreign Affairs

Released: 1977
Label: Elektra/Asylum
Producer: Bones Howe
Engineers: Bones Howe, Geoff Howe
Recorded: Filmways/Heider Recording, Hollywood,
July 28, August 2, 11, 12, 15, 1977

This is Waits at his most Lounge, a thoughtful, lyrically dense array of songs that may have benefited from more light interludes. 'Potter's Field' and 'Burma Shave' show Waits' dramatic, narrative gift, and his tender ear for human conversation is touchingly illustrated by 'Sight For Sore Eyes'.

Cinny's Waltz

Takes over where the theme from *Closing Time* leaves off, sweeping, oceanic strings that threaten to break into 'Ferry 'Cross The Mersey'.

Muriel

The persona from *Closing Time*'s 'Martha' is back again, this time playing one of the more expensive Holiday Inn lounges. A song that would sit well with the early solo-period Scott Walker.

I Never Talk To Strangers

The sainted Bette Midler asks the bartender for a Manhattan with prim coquettish perfection, and this duet between Bette and Tom can do no wrong. Midler's oddly sweet slipping around a woozy jazz scale is just what's needed to leaven Waits' after-hours grumbling.

Medley: Jack And Neal/California, Here I Come

A tribute to his Beat mentors, Kerouac and Cassady, which seems a little out of place and lacking in snap, although the song's coda, a brief rendering of 'California, Here I Come' makes its point very nicely.

A Sight For Sore Eyes

Takes on the tone of a Dickensian street sage, a sort of kindliness has begun to temper the streetwise melancholic. A crystalline piano drifting into 'Auld Lang Syne' lends a Christmassy musical-box air to the song. Old friends meet at the bar and exchange news about old times and the kind of old friend who dies in a car crash with the radio on.

Potter's Field

An eccentric orchestral soundscape, composed by the song's arranger, Bob Alcivar. Rolling waves of Leonard Bernstein-like drama tower and cower most wonderfully, as Waits barks an epic, cautionary fiction, populated by the usual fugitive ne'er-do-well and the occasional dangerous siren: 'he caught the cruel and unusual punishment of her smile'. Some exquisite clarinet from Gene Cipriano makes for another mini-masterpiece.

Burma Shave

A hoodlum-and-smalltown girl variation on 'Potter's Field'. A young punk on the run picks up a girl going crazy for something, just drive she said and, well, they never make it to Burma Shave. Sorry, did you expect them to find a nice house overlooking the golf course?

Barber Shop

A welcome three-minutes-and-fifty-two-seconds of insinuating levity: 'Good mornin' Mr Snip, Snip, Snip'. Conversations from the barber's chair over a playful drum 'n' bass jazz shuffle.

Foreign Affair

A quite charming discourse on itinerant yearnings, voiced by a man who sounds like he uses multi-syllabic words to play for time. It certainly begs for some sort of Dick Van Dyke-style interpretation, aided and abetted by cartoon woodland creatures drawn in blue.

Blue Valentine

Released: 1978
Label: Elektra
Producer: Bones Howe

Engineers: Bones Howe, Geoff Howe and Ralph Osborne
Recorded: Filmways/Heider Recording, Hollywood,
July 24, 25, August 10, 17, 23, 26, 1978

*This is a superb collection of songs, although the album
has been criticized as being more of the same, probably
because 'Romeo Is Bleeding' and 'Sweet Little Bullet
From A Pretty Blue Gun' take Waits two songs over his
Lifetime Beat Quota. However, the black humorous
appeal of these numbers should not be dismissed. The
old down-at-heel urban themes prevail and jazz-blues is
the main musical vehicle. This time, the depth and sadness conveyed by Waits' verse is more rooted in personal observation.* Blue Valentine *is a little more blues-
heavy than prior releases, and hints at the fun to come
on* Heartattack And Vine.

Somewhere

Another rare cover song, it begins with the blithe sophistication of
Hollywood Musical strings introducing this song from *West Side
Story*. Enter Waits, grunting and lisping in a touching fashion.

Red Shoes By The Drugstore

Darkly dramatic drums rumble in a most mysterioso mode, and a
girl keeps vigil for her beau. Unbeknownst to her, he was taken care
of whilst stealing something pretty for his baby. Waits paints a
poignant picture of a city street in the rain, people crowded at a bus
stop, 'umbrellas arranged in a sad bouquet'. Poor girl, she brought a
suitcase, and wore the red shoes he liked so much.

Christmas Card From A Hooker In Minneapolis

A great favourite and for good reason. A girl writes to an old friend,

Charlie, putting on a brave face, 'I think I'm happy for the first time since my accident'. This song is a fine example of Waits' ability to imply a multitude of personal histories in a three-sentence exchange. Just as we start to feel glad that she's pulled her life together, the chick hits up Charlie for money to make bail. All's well with the world.

Romeo Is Bleeding

Waits has said this was inspired by an ill-advised visit to buy something from a career criminal. 'Romeo is bleeding, but not so as you'd notice. 'Waits recalls that the man had suffered a shotgun wound but didn't want to ruin his reputation by doing anything about it in front of his henchmen and here he expertly conveys the stifled disbelief of the civilian observer. Surreal gangster poetry. Romeo repairs to a movie theatre to die.

$29.00

Sputtering lowdown blues, 'all you got is $29.00 and an alligator purse'. Another poor child, out too late in a place she don't belong, this one has a broken shoe and still believes in strangers. She just scrapes through an encounter with the Grim Reaper. Several lines are devoted to complaining about the police with little regard for scansion or poetry. It's not clear if it's Waits or the song speaking.

Wrong Side Of The Road

More dense sinister blues, sung in a masterful and most melodic growl.

Whistlin' Past The Graveyard

Boris Karloff meets Howlin' Wolf. Here, Waits shows a studied grasp of the blues idiom, with his fiendish, clotted growl, rearing up to a romping twelve-bar chorus. This song is a rare, lighthearted break. Screamin' Jay Hawkins, not surprisingly, covered it in the mid-1990s.

Kentucky Avenue

As sad as 'Graveyard' is silly, a five-Kleenex weepie. Waits' sentimental eye is just as keen when observing children as it is old drunks. A
dream of boyhood mischief and adventure, making up stories about
the neighbours, jumping off roofs. The singer dreams of rewriting the
sadness and pain, making it all right for his friend, who, we find out
in the last verse, cannot get out of his wheelchair to join in. This
elaborate last verse acts as a kind of magical spell: they'll take a hack-
saw to the friend's leg braces and bury them out in a cornfield and
he'll be borne aloft on magpie's wings and wheelchair spokes. The
song slips away in fantasy, so gently and so beautifully.

A Sweet Little Bullet From A Pretty Blue Gun

More archly strutting blues. The Cramps based a good part of their
grand career on this hiply syncopated nightmare muddle of
Americana.

Blue Valentines

A rare love song written in the first person, sung with a surprisingly mellifluous nod to jazz pin-up Chet Baker over a bare, blue elec-
tric guitar. Quite lovely.

Heartattack And Vine

Released: 1980
Label: Elektra
Producer: Bones Howe
Engineers: Bones Howe, Geoff Howe
Recorded: Filmways/Heider Studio B, Hollywood June 16
through July 15, 1980

The blues angle suggested by Blue Valentine *is most deliberately and heavily played here. Amongst the weighty guitar licks are several sentimental jewels.*

Heartattack And Vine

The birth of grunge-blues, this must have made a young Nick Cave very happy. 'Better off in Iowa against your scrambled eggs/than crawling down Cahuenga on a broken pair of legs'. The man surely can express himself.

In Shades

A lip-curling, lowdown instrumental. Lead guitar by Roland Bautista with Ronnie Barron at the Hammond organ.

Saving All My Love For You

This would be a much requested end-of-a-long-night ballad were it not for little details like 'I paid fifteen dollars for a prostitute/with too much make-up and a broken shoe'. Broken shoes, broken hearts – Waits feels your pain.

Downtown

Fraternal twin of 'Spooky'. Guttural and groovy. Oh, to hear Georgie Fame and Alan Price go to work on this one.

Jersey Girl

Almost a moon-in-June pop-rock crush song, but Waits still manages to warp it with a spectacular and joyous sha-la-la chorus that sounds like Van Morrison getting his teeth pulled. Next to this, Bruce Springsteen's version sounds quite demure.

'Til The Money Runs Out

'I sold a quart of blood and bought a half a pint of Scotch'. A really desperate 'Shakin' All Over' kind of vibe.

On The Nickel

A fine example of Waits' heartstring-tugging vaudeville. A gentle, avuncular, Dickensian character looks down on the lost boys on the street, the ones who have grown old and are sleeping rough. A companion to 'Kentucky Avenue' in the way it tries to rewrite sorrowful events into childish fantasy.

Mr Siegal

More dense blues and hefty roaring.

Ruby's Arms

'I will leave behind all my clothes/I wore when I was with you'. A sad slipping away at first light, hurrying past her broken window chimes and into a cheerless dawn. This has not been a very merry album at all.

One From the Heart (Original Soundtrack Recording)

Released: 1982
Label: CBS
Producer: Bones Howe
Engineers: Bones Howe, Biff Davies
Recorded: Wally Heider Recording, Hollywood

Waits duets with country chanteuse Crystal Gayle in his first full-length film soundtrack. Despite Gayle's pleasing clarity and vibrant vocal presence, her sobbing, almost resentful delivery is just a little too pouty at times. In the earlier songs, one misses the casual fluidity that Bette Midler brought to 'I Never Talk To Strangers'. Waits croons gently throughout.

Opening Montage – Tom's Piano Intro/Once Upon A Town/The Wages Of Love

Bob Alcivar returns with his swooping orchestra. Gayle and Waits duet.

Is There Any Way Out Of This Dream

Lazily melancholic cabaret number from Gayle with an exquisitely sheer sax solo from master player Teddy Edwards.

Picking Up After You

Bluesy duet from Gayle and Waits.

Old Boyfriends

'Old boyfriends lost in the pocket of your overcoat'. A lilting piece of jazz cabaret beautifully sung by Gayle.

Broken Bicycles

A little softer and more nostalgic language than we might be used to from Waits, but this does not detract from the excellence of the song, which is a very low-key Jacques Brel affair. Waits sings.

I Beg You Pardon

Tom softly whispers some Hoagy Carmichael lounge apologies.

Little Boy Blue

Swinging Waits jazz vocal with Ronnie Barron playing some impeccably tight organ swirls.

Instrumental Montage – The Tango/Circus Girl

Waits plays chunks of piano, possibly with his elbows, in an insistent tango fashion. 'Circus Girl' has Waits conducting an orchestra full of carnival motifs, a sound that would soon become very familiar.

You Can't Unring A Bell

A whispering sociopath ruminates over distant timpani. No, not Crystal Gayle.

This One's From The Heart

Gayle's high-end emoting works perfectly in this rippling lounge duet. Some pure and lovely trumpet from Jack Sheldon.

Take Me Home

More of a country feel allows Gayle to exit the album on a high note.

Presents

Glockenspiel and celeste tinkle in a short, pastel-coloured music-box theme.

Swordfishtrombones

Released: 1983
Label: Island
Producer: Tom Waits
Engineer: Biff Dawes
Recorded: Sunset Sound August 1982

The Germanic woofing of 'Underground' came as something of a jolt in 1983, after the old Waits was temporarily laid to rest. Then came the sheetmetal blues and bug-eyed calliopes. Life would never be the same.

Underground

'A theme for late-night activity in the steam tunnels', says Waits. A wonky urban fantasy of unseen city underworlds and northern european fairy tales.

Shore Leave

Waits envisaged this as a minor blues, a marine walking down a wet street in Hong Kong and missing his wife back home. Marimbas rumble like a low sky about to storm and the orchestra shifts in its seat. A whispered vocal lifts into an oddly sugary chorus. Brilliantly conceived.

Dave The Butcher

'I don't think it's going to get a lot of airplay. Unless we put a nice vocal on it.' Waits creates a nightmare carnival piece to depict a deeply religious acquaintance who spends his days working in a slaughterhouse.

Johnsburg, Illinois

A short, sweet, loving statement. 'Here's her picture.' Waits in rare straightforward mode, singing in a gentle croon.

16 Shells From A Thirty-Ought-Six

An inside-out blues groove that anticipates the grunge-funk of *Bone Machine*. Beefheart discotheque music where Tom lays down the funkified law.

Town With No Cheer

Wheezing bagpipes and mad attic harmonium paint a scene of faded desolation in an old Australian town: 'no spirits, no bilgewater, and 80 dry locals'.

Waits is very much the eccentrics' eccentric. Seen here with legendary misfit, Phil Ochs (above far right) and Beat guru Allan Ginsberg (below, centre)

Above and below Waits' days at the Tropicana Motel were seen through a haze of cigarette smoke or the bottom of a glass.

Above One suspects that on this occasion it is not just the piano that has been drinking.

Right Rickie Lee Jones, Waits' longtime companion.

Above and below In-character histrionics have always been very much a part of the Waits stage persona.

Above Onstage preparations for his nascent film career.
Below Fumblin' with the Blues onstage c. 1984.

Above 1999: Waits manages to hide his jubilation at the success of his million-selling, Grammy-nominated album *Mule Variations*.

Tom Waits: A unique chronicler of American melancholy.

In The Neighborhood

An affectionate big brass band strikes up as Waits details quirks and complaints in a lusty-throated baritone.

Just Another Sucker On The Vine

A delicate little vaudeville harmonium piece gets the old-timers slow dancing.

Frank's Wild Years

Over an absurdly pleasant lounge-jazz backing Waits narrates in a fairly normal fashion the tale of wayward Frank. He was never the most ideal of neighbours. That was before he drove the nail through his wife's head and burnt down the house. This one's going to run and run.

Swordfishtrombones

'He came home from the war with a party in his head'. Mean-eyed marimbas punctuate an upside-down folk song with a pleasingly even metre.

Down, Down, Down

Rabid gospel-blues, with an intro that sounds like a bad accident at the Motown studios.

Soldier's Things

A softly-whispered, teary-voiced cataloguing of an old soldier's effects at a garage sale. One of Waits' all-time greats. He writes so well of the pathos of everyday material remnants whose owners have passed away. The song makes one realize how, unlike most younger songwriters who are preoccupied with their own longings and sorrows, Waits has devoted a lot of time to writing about older people, with empathy and respect.

Gin Soaked Boy

Grubby, bloody blues. Another disgruntled soldier, this one about to get out of military prison, rants at his beloved for fooling around.

Trouble's Braids

Waits lists a few of his favourite disused phrases over a 'Red Shoes By The Drugstore' psycho-drama drumtrack.

Rainbirds

A delicate instrumental, a little sunlight to illuminate the dark corners. Some watercolour cinema piano clears a gentle space and we can all go home and dream nice dreams.

Rain Dogs

Released: 1985
Label: Island
Producer: Tom Waits
Engineer: Robert Musso
Recorded: RCS Studios, New York

If Swordfishtrombones *was middle-aged men and dusty streets,* Rain Dogs *is a lunatic voyage through every tale ever told to frighten children. The most polished production of all the albums, it gives the songs the space they need. Despite the unorthodox instrumentation, this is a pop album and a world music album. An absolute five-star must-buy, these songs are national treasures.*

Singapore

Lotte Lenya as head of the press gang sent by the carnival pirate ship to pick up wayward boys.

Clap Hands

Urgh. It's dark and dripping rain inside this Chinese Dragon suit and, oh, I don't think that's rain. A brilliantly disdainful guitar solo is the perfect compliment to this fearsome nonsense poem.

Cemetery Polka

Waits claims his mother called him to complain about his portrayal of Uncle Biltmore who, along with Uncle William, 'made a million during World War II but they're tightwads/And they're cheapskates/and they'll never give a dime to you'. Fact or fiction, Uncle Biltmore is a state of mind. A good song to sing whilst walking the plank.

Jockey Full Of Bourbon

A sheer growl over a dazzling bossa rhumba with Marc Ribot's torridly angular guitar syncopations. One of the top ten best ever guitar solos. 'Hey little bird fly away home' – nursery rhymes are suddenly fun again, even when they're scary.

Tango 'Til They're Sore

You always knew The Sandman had a day job as a vicious, murderous lounge singer.

Big Black Mariah

Larynx-ripping blues, a break from the Disney Hellride and, still, you can't stop singing along.

Diamonds & Gold
It's summer in Santa's cave and they've got the window open. Little pieces of *Mary Poppins*' 'Chim-Chiminee' drift in and out of this hobo's eulogy.

Hang Down Your Head
A doleful Celtic folk-rocker co-written with Kathleen Brennan. Sheer loveliness.

Time
If Tom's songs were priests, this one would be the Pope. A Leonard Cohen-like vocal over an acoustic guitar.

Rain Dogs
An Arabic flourish welcomes another Bavarian-style rocker via an antique Chinese port. Allegedly refers to dogs caught in the rain, whose scent trails are washed away, leaving them lost and disoriented. Waits' truest fans have adopted the name for themselves.

Midtown
The uptown horns dazzle us with some more Bernstein-and-a-switchblade jazz shapes. Tumultuous and confusing, a shock of colour. What the heck was that?

9th & Hennepin
'All the donuts have names that sound like prostitutes'. A dry-throated narrative: 'they all started out with bad directions'. Over a spaciously atmospheric backing, Waits now uses less lyrical detail but still tells a killer tale.

Gun Street Girl
Sincere, dusty-shoed country-blues, Waits plays some tentative

banjo in a song that writhes in all the right places. Predates the updating of Sonny Terry/Brownie McGhee territory by Beck in the 1990s.

Union Square

Time to pay tribute to Chuck Berry – featuring Keith Richards, of course.

Blind Love

Keith Richards is back again for a country and western sad song, where he adds some of those magical distant (and improbably girly) background vocals that made the early Stones albums so great. Waits hardly ever uses backing singers, so this makes Richards' inclusion extra, extra special. Another of those Waits songs you hear for the first time with a sense of *déjà entendu*.

Walking Spanish

More blues, with John Lurie adding some spooked-out sax. The song itself, though, never seems to make it beyond the sum of its parts.

Downtown Train

Time-honoured, classic 1980s pop-rock. Rod Stewart had better thank Tom for his best song since he left The Faces.

Bride Of Rain Dog

Another of Waits' harmonium bonkerthons. Ralph Carney loses it on sax.

Anywhere I Lay My Head

Waits pretty much screams this but, in a perverse way, one can hear The Platters doing a nice celestial doo-wop version.

Frank's Wild Years

Released: 1987
Label: Island
Producer: Tom Waits
Engineers: Danny Leake, Biff Dawes
Recorded: Sunset Sound, Los Angeles, Sunset Sound Factory, Los Angeles, Universal Recording Corp., Chicago

Having exhausted nursery rhymes, jump-rope songs and Keith Richards in Rain Dogs, *Waits takes the next logical step. An Operachi Romantico In Two Acts, of course. Kathleen Brennan and Greg Cohen co-write. Said Waits about this, the third in the informal trilogy, 'Frank took of in* Swordfish..., *had a good time in* Rain Dogs *and he's all grown up in* Frank's Wild Years... *I didn't get everything out that I wanted but I made some minor breakthroughs for myself.' One of them was discovering the joy of singing through a battery-operated bullhorn. He never looked back. Each song, he hoped, would be a drama unto itself.*

Hang On St Christopher
A righteous, inverted James Brown spectacular with spot-on horn arrangements by Greg Cohen.

Straight To The Top (Rhumba)
A trad jazz bellowing accompanies the band as they fall downstairs but keep on playing just the same.

Blow Wind Blow
Old man Caruso seems lost at the carnival. Although perturbed and

feeling a little teary, he seeks to convince anyone within a ten-mile radius he will be leaving any minute now.

Temptation

A blunt-topped rhumba with deep, deep roots. Waits sings in a gauzy falsetto. Brennan's vocal arrangements save a spot for some Arabic ululations amidst the bluesy hissing.

Innocent When You Dream (Barroom)

Another song from 1853, this one a gently-hollered waltz from the massed Tom Waits vocal orchestra.

I'll Be Gone

Waits saw this as some kind of Russian dance framing a flamboyant departure. Add the now-panicked Caruso on vocals and that's what you've got.

Yesterday Is Here

Another great track, a mutated Irish folk song as it would have been sung by Gordon Lightfoot. 'Today's gray skies/Tomorrow is tears/ You'll have to wait 'til yesterday is here.' Waits says actor Fred Gwynne gave him the title when they worked together on the film *The Cotton Club*.

Please Wake Me Up

Somebody is crooning sweetly in 1922, and somehow Waits has managed to record him.

Frank's Theme

Another delightful lullaby trembles around an antediluvian fair-ground organ.

More Than Rain
Tom does a butch and brave Edith Piaf and it sounds just right.

Way Down In The Hole
More wonderful chirruping horns from Greg Cohen over a skeletal Famous Flames backing track. Three female backing singers get to go 'oooh' for about one and a half seconds. That's it. One and a half seconds of female background singers going 'oooh' in a recording career of almost thirty years.

Straight To The Top (Vegas)
Disconcertingly accurate Tony Bennett swingalong number sung by Tom. Hmmm.

I'll Take New York
Waits carries over the Sinatra thing and it melts slowly into the mad Caruso voice.

Telephone Call From Istanbul
Nice little bit of Turkish banjo, but things aren't looking that good for Frank. Ends with dazzling shards of the antique organ.

Cold Cold Ground
Of all the songs Waits has ever written, this is one that would have been great for Elvis, around his 'Long Black Limousine' era, when his voice was starting to crack but he sang like he meant it more than ever.

Train Song
Come to think of it, this would be a great one for Elvis too. A slow gospel repentance song.

Innocent When You Dream (78)

Same song as before, this time sung solo by Waits with a hint of a German accent, and processed through an old 78 record effect. Marlene Dietrich never sounded better.

Big Time

Released: 1988
Label: Island
Producers: Tom Waits and Kathleen Brennan
Engineer: Biff Dawes
Recorded: Live, Los Angeles, San Francisco, Dublin, Stockholm, Berlin

16 Shells From A Thirty-Ought-Six/Red Shoes/ Underground/Cold Cold Ground/Straight To The Top/Yesterday Is Here/Way Down In The Hole/ Falling Down*/Strange Weather*/Big Black Mariah/ Rain Dogs/Train Song/Johnsburg, Illinois/Ruby's Arms/Telephone Call From Istanbul/Clap Hands/ Gun Street Girl/Time

* new songs

One very handy thing for Tom Waits is that he really doesn't have to worry much about reproducing his studio sound in a live concert environment and having it sound flat. 'Cold Cold Ground' actually seems to have more clarity when it's out of the Frank's Wild Years *theatrical setting. With the exception of 'Ruby's Arms', 'Red Shoes' and the two new songs, these are all songs from the* Swordfishtrombones *trilogy. The version of 'Straight To*

The Top' is the gospel shouter rhumba version, which is a pity as the camp Sinatra version would have added a little levity to the occasion. 'Yesterday Is Here' is a delicate, clippity-clop version which goes nicely into 'Way Down In The Hole'. 'Rain Dogs' acts as a big brother to 'Strange Weather' and is followed by Waits telling a little joke, a little risqué but a long way from the naughty-mouthed daddio on Nighthawks. *The other songs are rendered sincerely and faithfully, finishing with the sublime 'Time'. However, when it comes to spending your money, spend more and buy all three of the* Swordfishtrombones *trilogy because there are songs like 'Soldiers Things', 'Hang Down Your Head' and 'Hang On St Christopher' that you can't afford to miss. If you can only buy one, it' a tough decision but you'd do best going for the Island compilation,* Beautiful Maladies, *and you are going to have to get 'Ruby's Arms' some other way.*

Falling Down

Upright church harmonium frames Waits' very passable Mick Jagger voice in the verse. An agonized chorus hints at 'Cold Cold Ground' and 'Train Song'.

Strange Weather

Marlene Dietrich returns for an archly classy promenade through weird shadows. Most accomplished.

The Early Years Volumes 1 and 2

Released: 1991
Label: Manifesto (Bizarre/Straight)

Producer: Robert Duffey
Engineer: Robert DeMars
Recorded: July–September 1971, Los Angeles, CA

The following two releases are the early demos Waits did not want released.

With the exception of the ludicrous 'Had Me A Girl' and the clear country parody 'Looks Like I'm Up Shit Creek Again', the songs on Volume 1 are not really dreadful, they simply lack distinction when compared to the visceral depth of the artist's later work. Many struggling songwriters may even find it encouraging that the same mind that composed the tragically obser- vant 'Small Change' could blithely rhyme 'Tallahassee' and 'Foxy lassie' ('Had Me A Girl'). There are those amongst us, true lovers of Tom Waits, who can be brought to shivering peaks of ecstasy just hearing his chair creak. These people, and compulsive completist collectors, are the target audience for Volume 1. There are others who will deny themselves these rare climac- tic pleasures since they feel they'd be violating Tom, who didn't want them to hear these recordings. They might want to rethink their purchasing position regarding Volume 2, which is by far the superior. Some endearing simple interpretations of old favourites and some gently insidious 'new' ones.

VOLUME 1

Goin' Down Slow
Easygoing New Orleans blues, very late period, casual Clapton.

Poncho's Lament

Tremulous country. 'So I'll throw another log on the fire/And I'll admit that I'm a lousy liar', confides Cowboy Tom.

I'm Your Late Night Evening Prostitute

'Drink your martini and stare at the moon/Don't mind me, I'll continue to croon'. Somewhat endearing facetiousness, given the Billy Joel-like setting of the song.

Had Me A Girl

No one would ever guess this was Tom Waits. Ever. Neither the voice nor the song bear any resemblance to the man who made *Closing Time*, let alone *Swordfishtrombones*.

Ice Cream Man

Somewhat slower version of the song that appeared on *Closing Time*.

Rockin' Chair

Along the lines of 'Goin' Down Slow'.

Virginia Avenue

Quite recognizable as the song appearing on *Closing Time*.

Midnight Lullabye

As is this.

When You Ain't Got Nobody

Slow-rolling good-time piano blues.

Little Trip To Heaven

Appears on *Closing Time*. Great song.

Frank's Song

More Tin Pan Alley piano blues.

Looks Like I'm Up Shit Creek Again

Silly country rock. Nice melody. It would have been fun to hear the Eagles do this one.

So Long I'll See Ya

Gritty vocal, plaintive scat singing, the song is a pale version of the Tom Waits to come.

VOLUME 2

Hope I Don't Fall In Love With You

A sweet song, the guitar intro always threatening to break into 'Tracks of My Tears'. From *Closing Time*.

Ol' 55

Very tentative version of the *Closing Time* opener. Some might appreciate the barer treatment, minus the harmonies and stream-rollering piano.

Mockin' Bird

One of the rare unrecorded gems. Love the out-of-tune whistling solo and the John Prine vibe.

In Between Love

Another contemplative country-folk song with unusual shadings.

Blue Skies

A less viscous James Taylor thing.

Nobody

Shaky, oddly soothing bluesy swing.

I Want You

A rather silly song.

Shiver Me Timbers

His voice lacks the depth of the version on *Heart Of Saturday Night*.

Grapefruit Moon

Milky, somewhat slurred version, less pert than the one on *Closing Time*, which works much better for this song.

Diamonds On My Windshield

A more syncopated vocal than the officially recorded version, without the Beat drama.

Please Call Me, Baby

The official version has a little more verve.

So It Goes

Lovely Anglo-folk, another missing treasure.

Old Shoes

A nicely unadorned version of the song from Closing Time.

Bone Machine

Released: 1992
Label: Island
Producer: Tom Waits

Engineers: Biff Dawes, Joe Marquez, Michael Morris
Recorded: Prairie Sun Recording, Cotati, CA

A much more percussive, rhythmic venture. Lots of field holler and country blues, oil-can percussion and primitive rock. Waits has said the sounds conjured up 'wet leaves in your hair… autumn'. There is a very earthy death motif running through the songs, counterbalanced with some simple church spirituals and labour songs.

Earth Died Screaming

Waits, in a promotional interview sent out with the album, recalled a fellow who would stand at LA's Fifth and Main screaming about the end of the world through a little microphone and crappy speaker housed in a briefcase. To that memory, Waits adds a Native American feel. 'The earth died screaming/While I lay dreaming'.

Dirt In The Ground

A funereal sway of sax and such from Ralph gives a dusky setting for Waits' shredded treble. More death blues.

Such A Scream

A wild-eyed grunge cha-cha. Waits raises the spectre of Marc Ribot with his deliberate blocks of ragged guitar.

All Stripped Down

More of Waits' 'Prince Voice', which is just perfect for this funky little call-and-response adventure. Imagine master chef Julia Child getting a little carried away at Mardi Gras and you're right there.

Who Are You

A beautiful, cooling stream of a song, with an old-fashioned folk aspect to it, and verily the hand of Brennan is upon it.

The Ocean Doesn't Want Me

Waits alone with his Chamberlain muttering in a back-to-his-beginnings reverie. Enchanting, although it shouldn't be.

Jesus Gonna Be Here

Waits pays tribute to the Folkways series, sounding every bit like a seventy-year-old with calloused hands, recorded in his vegetable allotment. 'He's gonna cover us up with leaves/With a blanket from the moon.'

A Little Rain

Another contemplative piano song for the Disney movie that never was.

In The Colosseum

Great metal percussion, one of which is the excellently-named Conundrum. Sometimes, though, Waits takes the murderous, blood-curdling melodrama a little too far.

Goin' Out West

Eddie Cochran rises from the ashes of the car crash, and look out! He's still got one more song to sing. Joe Gore plays some badlands twang to great effect.

Murder In The Red Barn

Nightmare kitchen clippety-clopping: 'Is that blood on the tree/Or is it autumn's red blaze?' An exquisite couplet, a Waits/Brennan collaboration.

Black Wings

A distant cousin of 'Jockey Full Of Bourbon' without the swirling skirts. Waits and Jim Jarmusch formed an informal club called The Sons of Lee Marvin, whose sole purpose is to watch Lee's movies. This would be its theme song, prime alt.country noir.

Whistle Down The Wind

Another tragic lament. David Hidalgo plays violin and accordion, David Phillips plays just enough pedal steel. 'someday I'd go/Where the blue-eyed girls/and red guitars and/naked rivers flow.' Perfect simplicity.

I Don't Wanna Grow Up

Busker with cymbals strapped to his knees sings for the kids at the birthday party. 'Is that really your Dad?' Brilliant.

Let Me Get Up On It

A brief blurt of primitive instrumental music.

That Feel

Co-written with Keith Richards, who also plays guitar alongside Waddy Wachtel and Waits. The song sways, anthem-like and with a strange fragility.

Night on Earth (Original Soundtrack Recording)

Released: 1992
Label: Island
Producer: Tom Waits
Engineers: Biff Dawes, Joe Marquez
Recorded: Prairie Sun Recording, Cotati, CA.

*The influence of the likes of Bob Alcivar ('Potter's Field')
can be heard in the sophisticated orchestration and sinister jazz motifs. A kind of Ellis Island family reunion for
the whole of America. Beautifully thought out and ten-
derly rendered.*

Back In The Good Old World (gypsy)

The vocal version, a fine approximation of an old European folk
song.

Los Angeles Mood (chromium descensions)

Francis Thumm at the Stinson band organ, the rest of the band pluck
away evenly at their pieces and Joe Gore splashes a little guitar
scree across the canvas.

Los Angeles Theme (another private dick)

Some good old 1950s mystery horns over a pre-Duane Eddy
guitar line. Beware, swarms of dissonant bees will infest your ears.

New York Theme (hey you can have that heartattack outside, buddy)

The LA mystery theme returns, this time slinking moodily over
some tinkling jazz piano.

New York Mood (a new haircut and a busted lip)

The same theme, this time sulking in a doorway.

Baby, I'm Not A Baby Anymore

Whoa, would you check out the vibrato on those horns. It's more
than a man can stand. Simple, colourful curves.

Good Old World (waltz)

Softly swaying, wobbling gently, the old yellowed photographs in the family album start to make their music heard.

Carnival (Brunello Del Montalcino)

A happy nightmare winding through the funfair.

On The Other Side Of The World (vocal)

'And she tastes of the sea/And she's waiting for me'. A quaint little French thing, mostly, except for conversation-stopping lines like 'should I shave/or end it all?'

Good Old World (gypsy instrumental)

The yellowed old family photographs are now in the living room and have invited their friends over. Sweet, distant jollity.

Paris Mood (un de fromage)

The main theme as rendered by innocent bystanding accordions. Un de fromage, indeed.

Dragging A Dead Priest

Exactly what it sounds like.

Helsinki Mood

Ah, Helsinki, poster child of cold war 1960s intrigue. Interestingly, this most singular of European cities is here characterized by some lightly psychotic klezmer music.

Carnival Bob's Confession

'Helsinki Mood' as seen through the Hall of Mirrors.

Good Old World (waltz) (vocal)
More softly sentimental memoirs from a grizzled old boy.

On The Other Side Of The World (instrumental)
A late afternoon's dallying in some Mediterranean secret spot. Charming. Let's hope the tour buses never find it.

The Black Rider

Released: 1993
Label: Island
Producer: Tom Waits
Engineers: Tchad Blake, Joe Marquez
(USA) Gerd Bessler (Germany)
Recorded: Prairie Sun recording Studios, Cotati, CA, USA
Music Factory, Hamburg, Germany

A German folk operetta may not sound like the most inviting of purchases, but this beautifully voiced and arranged selection of songs is one of Waits' best creations. His love of the Weill/Brecht era of cabaret is apparent, and the guest vocal of William S Burroughs is a glorious thing. Musical direction and co-arranging of the work in Germany was undertaken by longtime colleague Greg Cohen. Kathleen Brennan and Francis Thumm are also credited with various degrees of direction and production. The play was a collaboration with playwright Robert Wilson.

Lucky Day Overture
Over beauteously executed Weimar brass, Waits barks his freak-

sodden lunacy and gives shrieking US comedian Gilbert Gottfried a run for his money with the tonsil-ripping introduction. You wouldn't dare ignore this invitation.

The Black Rider
Rowdy *Threepenny Opera* knees-up. You are dared not to sing along.

November
Thoughtful, delightful autumnal musings with a marvellously placed musical saw, played by Don Neely. 'Send word to April to rescue me'.

Just The Right Bullets
Vicious and dastardly, mean and evil, something is slinking across the Cabaret stage.

Black Box Theme
The musical saw is back, rain-streaked horns and looming bassoons. No vocal. Delightful.

T'Ain't No Sin
A song written by Walter Donaldson and Edgar Leslie and sung by old Bill Burroughs, famous literary junkie and cat-lover.

Flash Pan Hunter/Intro
An instrumental played by the German end of the project, Henning Stoll (contra bassoon), Stefan Schäfer (bass) and Volker Hemken (clarinet). It bleeds into the next song where they are joined by…

That's The Way
… Hans-Jörn Braudenberg on organ, and Burroughs on sinister recital.

The Briar And The Rose

The German woodwind and organ section drift sweetly behind Waits' sentimental wheezing. A sweetheart of a song, written, no doubt, for the lovely Kathleen.

Russian Dance

A bright-eyed, boot-stomping trip back to the Old Country with Slavic fiddles and a playfully revived diminuendo.

Gospel Train/Orchestra

The Americans interpret the lurching dissonant instrumental. Not for those with a pre-existing nauseous condition.

I'll Shoot The Moon

An amusingly morbid Tony-Bennett-in-hell sort of love song: 'I'll be the pennies on your eyes for you, baby'. A good opportunity to stay home and wash your hair, girls.

Flash Pan Hunter

A Waits/Burroughs collaboration with more of Don Neely's wonderful saw.

Crossroads

Waits sings Burroughs words again, as a kind of northern European, half-remembered cowboy dream. The Chamberlain provides some ghostly Joe Meekery with its backing 'vocal'.

Gospel Train

Waits gets to indulge his love of train whistles. Again the sickly and their jittery pets are advised to move on to the next track. Waits sings.

Interlude

A thirty-second Greg Cohen composition. Christoph Moinian adds french horn to some clarinet and bassoon.

Oily Night

Satan has a bout of nasty heartburn during a runaway train instrumental. Frighteningly lifelike.

Lucky Day

Ah, that's better. An old European honey of a ballad. Waits roars his best impression of a cranky old bandleader with a Lotte Lenya fixation.

The Last Rose Of Summer

Gently seeping strings and woodwind (actually, it's the Chamberlain again) ripple like thin curtains across a window. 'I love the way/the tattered clouds/go wind across the sky.' A pretty, pretty song.

Carnival

Tom, Greg and the Chamberlain give it their best. German carnival collides with whistling steam engine. No singing.

Mule Variations

Released: 1999
Label: Epitaph
Producers: Tom Waits and Kathleen Brennan
Engineers: Oz Fritz, Jacquire King, Jeff Sloan, Gene Cornelius
Recorded: Prairie Sun Recording Studios/Sputnik Sound

This was voted the independent radio album of the year by the US radio industry monitor GAVIN, and for good reason. This is a distillation of everything Waits has ever done, and all the gang, old and new, are here (with the exception of maybe old Chuck E): Marc Ribot, Smokey Hormel, Larry Taylor, Les Claypool, Ralph Carney and more. The credits include programming and DJ action, but this is interwoven almost imperceptibly. In contrast to the sometimes bleak Bone Machine, this is a warm and sentimental collection. An indispensable acquisition. Despite the deep and old-fashioned folk foundations, Mule Variations defies categorization. Some non-USA releases contain two extra songs, 'Big Face Money' and 'Buzz Flederjohn'.

Big In Japan
Amidst the crashing of metal sheets and semi-Devo groove, Waits pukes a malevolently catchy pop song.

Lowside Of The Road
A hazy old country blues, dusty and gravel-laden. Smokey Hormel plays Chumbus and Dousengoni, whatever they are. Of course, that sort of thing is legal in California.

Hold On
Everyone who hears this hears Bruce Springsteen singing too. A gorgeous, gentle comfort song, co-written with Kathleen Brennan and, not surprisingly, the choice for a single. Stephen Hodges plays immaculate soft-focus percussion.

Get Behind The Mule
More funky blues in the field, repetitive and endearing.

House Where Nobody Lives

A sweetly sentimental meditation on real family values.

Cold Water

An infectious, slacker rock 'n' roll blues grind from the vaults of the American Nursery, except these hobo blues would be a touch too depressing for the kids: 'Pregnant women and Vietnam vets… beggin' on the freeway'.

Pony

Songs like this might be maudlin in other hands – the tired old wanderer reminiscing, hoping his old pony knows the way home – but Waits keeps it honest. The sweetness behind the sadness, a broken-down Burl Ives ballad.

What's He Building?

Another song where Waits mutters to himself whilst things fall, just because he can. Mr Sticha makes an appearance, peeking in the window of the neighbour who keeps himself to himself, the greatest of all neighbourhood sins. 'He has no friends/But he gets a lot of mail'.

Black Market Baby

The world's slowest horse ambles through them thar hills, pans and saddle clanking. Atop his lumbering mount, Lee Marvin's batteries are running low.

Eyeball Kid

A fantasy fable about Waits' other great love, the circus oddity who shows us the truth. A nutty metal-banging cacophony.

Picture In A Frame

Sometimes one suspects songs like 'Eyeball Kid' exist just to show off the pretty lines and tender corners of songs like this. He makes the line 'I love you baby and I always will' shimmer with sincerity.

Chocolate Jesus

A quiet, dulcet spiritual, singing the twin praises of the Lord and confectionery. Charlie Musselwhite contributes some soft-spoken harp. A tip-toeing lodger of a song.

Georgia Lee

A heartrending lament, 'Why wasn't God watching... for Georgia Lee?' Another too-short childhood.

Filipino Box Spring Hog

A raucous slammer inspired, it's said, by the day they tossed the mattress on the bonfire chez Waits. 'Kathleen was sitting down... in her criminal underwear bra'. Just as you expected.

Take It With Me

Tom is just a great big softie with some bad tattoos and no amount of 'Eyeball Kids' can cover this up.

Come On Up To The House

Young record store clerk: 'Hey, *Black Rider*, that's a very cool album. Yeah, *Bone Machine* too... lots of pots and pans. *Mule Variations*? I dunno, I mean... (sings) "Come on up to the house"??(looks bewildered and appalled)... what's that? it sounds like somebody's Dad.' The record store clerk will come around one day. This beauteous, raggedy hymn seeks to include all. Wonderful.

COMPILATIONS

TRIBUTE ALBUMS

Step Right Up: The Songs Of Tom Waits

Manifesto, 1995

Drugstore: Old Shoes/Tindersticks: Mockin' Bird/
Pete Shelley: Better Off Without A Wife/The
Wedding Present: Red Shoes By The Drugstore/
Violent Femmes: Step Right Up/Alex Chilton:
Downtown/Archers Of Loaf: Big Joe And Phantom
309/These Immortal Souls: You Can't Unring A Bell/
Jeffrey Lee Pierce: Pasties And A G-String/
Magnapop: Christmas Card From A Hooker In
Minneapolis/Dave Alvin: Ol' 55/Pale Saints: Jersey
Girl/ Tim Buckley: Martha/Frente: Ruby's Arms/
10,000 Maniacs: I Hope That I Don't Fall In Love
With You

New Coat of Paint: The Songs Of Tom Waits

Manifesto 2000

Screamin' Jay Hawkins: Whistlin' Past The Graveyard/
Andre Williams: Pasties And A G-String/Lydia Lunch
featuring Nels Cline: Heartattack And Vine/Knoxville
Girls: Virginia Avenue/Dexter Romweber's Infernal
Racket: Romeo Is Bleeding/Lee Rocker: New Coat
Of Paint/Botanica: Broken Bicycles/Preacher Boy:
Old Boyfriends/Sally Norvell: Please Call Me,

Baby/Carla Bozulich: On The Nickel/Eleni Mandell:
Muriel/The Blacks: Poncho's Lament/Neko Case:
Christmas Card From A Hooker In Minneapolis/
Floyd Dixon: Blue Skies

*These two collections from Manifesto Records are all
compiled from the Herb Cohen/Elektra era of Waits'
song collection, so you'll find nothing from*
Swordfishtrombones *onward.* New Coat Of Paint *is
hipper, with more artists attuned to the Waits wave-
length and acknowledging a clear Waits influence in
their work. These include the old Birthday Party/Lydia
Lunch school and the alt.Americana people, plus a
handful of old-time blues and jazz artists.* Paint *is also
the better album, in terms of flow and consistency.* Step
Right Up *demonstrates that Waits' songs can be performed by pretty much anyone, and there are several
outstanding performances. The Violent Femmes are
clearly cut from the same cloth as Tom. Their rendition of
'Step Right Up' (did they mail dead creeping charlies to
get the words?) transports the voice of the original
hawker twenty-odd years into the future. Gordon Gano's
mad mutterings has the hustler talking to himself,
shrieking bitterly, perhaps having decided there's no one
else listening. The band's Brian Ritchie notes in the liner
notes that Waits refused a job producing them, so they
were repaying the compliment by 'mutilating' one of
Waits' compositions. A very Waitsian comment. Tim
Buckley's 'Martha' is a fabulous epic taking up where
Tom left off, and the Pale Saints' version of 'Jersey Girl' is
a thing of beauteous psychedelic gossamer. Jeffrey Lee
Pierce shifts the jazz shuffle of 'Pasties' to a rap groove*

and works it brilliantly. Andre Williams also takes the song on 'Paint' and pushes it into a more dancehall/industrial dub domain which is also fun. A curious inclusion on Step Right Up is 'Big Joe And Phantom 309' which was not written by Waits at all, although he did a memorable version of the song. Nighthawks At The Diner credits the writer as Tommy Faile, and the publisher as Fort Knox Music. Now Manifesto credits the song under the Fifth Floor Music umbrella.

Not surprisingly, both albums feature a version of 'Christmas Card From A Hooker …' a song that is lyrically rich but possesses a melody that could turn tedious in inexperienced hands. It needs a vocalist with strong timbre and phrasing. Both Magnapop and Neko Case fulfil the necessary criteria. Magnapop's contribution is a kooky groaner, with a strung out, sexy delivery from Linda Hopper, dramatically mannered stuff that only an American could pull off. Case goes for a more straightforward chanteusey tragi-chat, which is also excellent. Finally, although it may have diehard Rain Dogs reaching for the smelling salts, it must be said that Lydia Lunch's interpretation of 'Heartattack And Vine' is even better than Tom Waits'. She was born to do this song, and ever since the release of 'Queen Of Siam' at the turn of the 1980s, has always had similar sensibilities, even when tripping through the outer regions of post punk New York performance art.

Both collections step out of the jazz/Euro cabaret field, which may alienate a few Waits fans, but both are very entertaining albums.

Holly Cole
Temptation

Metro Blue/Capitol, 1995

Take Me Home/Train Song/Jersey Girl/Temptation/
Falling Down/Invitation To The Blues/Cinny's Waltz/
Frank's Theme/Little Boy Blue/I Don't Wanna Grow
Up/Tango 'Til They're Sore/(Looking For) The Heart
Of Saturday Night/Soldiers Things/I Want You/Good
Old World/The Briar And The Rose

*This is certainly a favourite amongst Rain Dogs. Cole
and her trio have selected a perfectly obvious/not-obvi-
ous selection of songs and have made a wondrous
album. Her vocal style, a slightly slurred, under-the-
weather (but always spot-on pitch) Annette Peacock,
has a dark narcotic quality that will appeal to both a
jazz vocal audience and everybody else. A welcome
addition is her trio's interpretation of the lovely instrumental theme 'Cinny's Waltz'. Sometimes, listening to
'Jersey Girl' or 'Tango 'Til They're Sore', you miss the
straight lines and familiar planes of Waits' melodies, for
Cole likes to dismantle and slide the phrases around the
scale, but her vocal timbre is so easy on the ear that you
have to surrender all memory of the original song.
Another bold move is to choose the kiddie tantrum song
'I Don't Wanna Grow Up' and turn it into a pouty siren
song. She takes '(Looking For) The Heart Of Saturday
Night' and carries it into her upper register, which turns
out to be a beautifully pure country voice. Both Holly
Cole and her band have truly absorbed the essence of
the songs and they execute them with confidence. They*

have smoothed out the eccentric elements that some-times make Waits' songs uneasy listening, but have retained the other-worldly weirdness and sensuality. You don't even have to like Tom Waits to own this album.

COMPILATIONS OF TOM WAITS' RECORDINGS

Bounced Checks

Asylum, 1981 (out of print)

Heartattack And Vine/Jersey Girl/Eggs And Sausage/ I Never Talk To Strangers/The Piano Has Been Drinking (live in Dublin)/Whistling Past The Graveyard/Mr Henry/Diamonds On My Windshield/Burma Shave/Tom Traubert's Blues

This out-of-print compilation contains the previously unreleased track 'Mr Henry', a delightful little story about a man tottering home, a little the worse for wear.

Anthology

WEA/Elektra, 1985

Ol' 55/Diamonds On My Windshield/(Looking For) The Heart Of Saturday Night/I Hope That I Don't Fall In Love With You/Martha/Tom Traubert's Blues/The Piano Has Been Drinking/I Never Talk To Strangers/Somewhere/Burma Shave/Jersey Girl/San

Diego Serenade/Sight For Sore Eyes

The Asylum Years

Asylum, 1986 (CD version)

Diamonds On My Windshield/(Looking For) The
Heart Of Saturday Night/Martha/The Ghosts Of
Saturday Night (After Hours At Napoleone's Pizza
House)/Grapefruit Moon/Small Change/Burma
Shave/I Never Talk To Strangers/Tom Traubert's
Blues/Blue Valentines/Potter's Field/Kentucky
Avenue/Somewhere/Ruby's Arms

Beautiful Maladies

Island, 1998

Hang On St Christopher/Temptation/Clap Hands/
The Black Rider/Underground/Jockey Full Of
Bourbon/Earth Died Screaming/Innocent When You
Dream (78)/Straight To The Top (Rhumba)/Frank's
Wild Years (For Frankie Z)/Singapore/Shore Leave/
Johnsburg, Illinois/Way Down In The Hole/Strange
Weather (live)/Cold Cold Ground (live)/November/
Downtown Train/Sixteen Shells From A Thirty-
Ought-Six/Jesus Gonna Be Here/Good Old World
(Waltz)/I Don't Wanna Grow Up/Time

*Selected by Waits himself from the Island releases of
1982–1993. Fabulous.*

SINGLES

Ol' 55
Asylum, 1973
(Looking For) The Heart Of Saturday Night
Asylum, 1974
Blue Skies/New Coat Of Paint
Asylum, 1974
San Diego Serenade
Asylum, 1974
Step Right Up/The Piano Has Been Drinking
Asylum, 1976
Somewhere/Red Shoes By The Drugstore
Elektra/Asylum, 1979
Jersey Girl/Heartattack And Vine
Elektra/Asylum, 1980
In The Neighborhood/Frank's Wild Years
Island, 1983
Downtown Train/'Tango Till They're Sore
Island, 1985
Downtown Train/'Tango Till They're Sore/Jockey Full Of Bourbon
Island, (12") 1985
NME'S Big Four – including 'Downtown Train'
(Special promotion) (1986)
In The Neighborhood/Singapore
Island, 1986
In The Neighborhood/Singapore/Tango Till They're Sore
(live)/Rain Dogs (live)
Island, 1986
In The Neighborhood/Jockey Full Of Bourbon/Tango Till They're
Sore (live)/16 Shells From A Thirty-Ought-Six (live)
Island, (12") 1986

Hang On St Christopher/Hang On St Christopher (instrumental)
Island, (12") 1987
16 Shells/Black Mariah/Ruby's Arms (live)
Island, (12") 1987
16 Shells From A Thirty-Ought-Six/Black Mariah (live)
Island, 1987
Goin' Out West/A Little Rain/The Ocean Doesn't Want Me/Back
in the Good Old World
UK Island, 1992
Goin' Out West
Island, 1992
Goin' Out West
Island 1992
Hold On
Epitaph, 1999

OTHER CONTRIBUTIONS

This list only includes recordings not available on the albums already
noted in main discography. Also includes musical performances and
interviews.

Broken Blossom – Bette Midler (1977)
Album: Played piano.

Homeplate – Bonnie Raitt (1977)
Album: Vocal and piano contribution to 'Your Sweet And Shiny Eyes'.

Jack Tempchin – Jack Tempchin (1977)
Album: co-wrote song contribution 'Tijuana'.

Paradise Alley – Directed by Sylvester Stallone (1978)
Film: Composer of songs 'Annie's Back In Town' and 'Paradise Alley'.

On The Nickel – Directed by Ralph Waites (1980)
Film: Composer of song 'On The Nickel' (original recording).

Poetry In Motion – Directed by Ron Mann (1982)
Film: Spoken word performance.

Girl At Her Volcano – Rickie Lee Jones (1983)
Album: Song contribution 'Rainbow Sleeves'.

Lost In The Stars – Various (1985)
Album: song contribution 'What Keeps Mankind Alive?' Songs of Kurt Weill, produced by Hal Willner.

Streetwise – Directed by Martin Bell (1985)
Film: Composer of songs 'Take Care Of All My Children' and 'Rat's Theme'.

Smack My Crack – Various (1987)
Album: spoken word 'The Pontiac'–Giorno Poetry Systems Records project.

Big Time – Directed by Chris Blum (1988)
Film: Tom Waits mostly live musical performance.

Roy Orbison And Friends – A Black And White Night (1988)
Film: Musical performance.

Stay Awake – Various (1989)

Album: song contribution 'Heigh Ho'. Songs from Disney movies, produced by Hal Willner.

Sea Of Love – Directed by Harold Becker (1989)

Film: Arranger of song 'Sea Of Love'.

Red Hot & Blue – Various (1990)

Album: Song 'It's Alright With Me'.

Mississippi Lad – Teddy Edwards (1991)

Album: Two song and vocal contributions, 'I'm Not Your Fool Anymore' and 'Little Man'.

Sailing The Seas Of Cheese – Primus (1991)

Album: Vocal contribution 'Tommy The Cat'.

American Heart – Directed by Martin Bell (1992)

Film: Composer of songs 'I'll Never Let Go Of Your Hand' and 'Jack's Flashback Scene', artist 'I'm Crazy 'Bout My Baby'.

Got Love If You Want It – John Hammond (1992)

Album: Song contribution 'No One Can Forgive Me'.

Devout Catalyst – Ken Nordine (1992)

Album: Spoken word contribution.

Coffee And Cigarettes: Somewhere In America – Directed by Jim Jarmusch (1993)

Film: discussion with Iggy Pop. Jarmusch assembled various personalities and asked them to discuss coffee and cigarettes.

Jesus' Blood Never Failed Me Yet – Gavin Bryars (1993)

Album: Vocal contribution.

Contemporary British composer Bryars first released his Jesus Blood project in the early 1970s. He had taped an older homeless man singing a short hymn and began to make a loop of the vocal at the art school where he taught. Having left the room whilst the tape was copying he returned to find the group of boisterous art students in the next room, weeping and solemn. Realizing the emotional impact of the tramp's voice, he composed an album around the vocal. The 1993 album is a revision of the original work featuring Waits singing with the tramp.

American Recordings – Johnny Cash (1994)

Album: Song contribution, 'Down There By The Train'.

Dead Man Walking – Directed by Tim Robbins (1996)

Film: Composer of songs 'Walk Away' and 'The Fall Of Troy' (with Kathleen Brennan).

The End Of Violence – Directed by Wim Wenders (1997)

Film: Composer of song 'Little Drop Of Poison'.

Waiting For Twilight (1997)

Documentary: Narrator.

Gravikords, Whirlies and Pyrophones – Bart Hopkin (1997)

Album and book: Waits wrote the foreword. A celebration of unorthodox musical instrumentation.

Bunny – Directed by Chris Wedge (1998)

Film: Composer of this Oscar-winning animated short's music with Kathleen Brennan.

Friends Of Mine – Ramblin' Jack Elliot (1998)

Album: Duet on song 'Louise'.

The Songs Of Kinky Friedman – Various (1998)

Album: Song, 'Highway Café'.

KCRW's Morning Becomes Eclectic 4 – Various (1998)

Album: Song, 'Fall Of Troy' (live).

Orbitones, Spoon Harps & Bellowphones – Bart Hopkin (1999)

Album: Song contribution. 'Babbachichuija' Follow-up to Gravikords, Whirlies and Pyrophones.

On The Road – Various With Jack Kerouac (1999)

Album: Song performance with Primus, 'On The Road'.

Extremely Cool – Chuck E Weiss (1999)

Album: Producer, vocals.

More 'Oar': A tribute to Alexander 'Skip' Spence – Various Artists (1999)

Album: song contribution, cover of Spence's 'Books Of Moses'.
A tribute to the former Jefferson Airplane drummer and Moby Grape guitarist in the form of assorted artists re-recording the songs from Spence's solo album Oar. The original work was released in 1969, after Spence had spent six month at Bellevue mental hospital. Its skeletal acid delta blues went unappreciated and it was said to be the lowest-selling album ever on Columbia Records. Sales were set at 700 copies. Spence's Oar sold much more when it was re-released almost twenty years later.

VH-1 feature as part of their 'Storytellers' series (June 1999)
Not commercially available.

Moanin' Parade: The Gatmo Sessions Volume 1 – C-Side/Petit Mal (2000)
Album guest: improvisations on this and on the next album, *Swarm Warnings*.

Helium – Tin Hat Trio (2000)
Album track vocal: 'Helium Reprise'.

Beatin' The Heat – Dan Hicks And The Hot Licks (2000)
Album: Vocal contribution, 'I'll Tell You What It Is'.

Liberty Heights – Directed by Barry Levinson (2000)
Film: Composer of songs 'Pulling On The Dog' and 'It's Over' (with Kathleen Brennan).

COVERS BY OTHER ARTISTS

This does not include tracks detailed in tribute albums above or tracks in other contributions.

The Eagles: 'Ol' 55' from the album *On The Border* (Asylum, 1974)
Ian Matthews: 'Ol' 55' from the album *Some Days You Eat Bear… And Some Days The Bear Eats You* (Elektra, 1974)
Eric Anderson: 'Ol' 55' from the album *Be True To You* (Arista, 1975)
Jerry Jeff Walker: '(Looking For) The Heart Of Saturday Night' from the album *It's A Good Night For Singing* (MCA, 1976)

Bette Midler: 'Shiver Me Timbers' from the album *Songs For The New Depression* (Atlantic, 1976)

Dion DiMucci: '(Looking For) The Heart Of Saturday Night' from the album *Return Of The Wanderer* (DCC Records, 1978)

Manhattan Transfer: 'Foreign Affair' from the album *Extensions* (Atlantic, 1980)

English Country Blues Band: 'Tom Traubert's Blues' from the album *Home And Deranged* (Rogue Records, 1983)

Bruce Springsteen: 'Jersey Girl' (live) from the 12'' single 'Cover Me' (CBS, 1984)

Beat Farmers: 'Rosie' from the album *The Pursuit Of Happiness* (Curb, 1987)

Mary Chapin Carpenter: 'Downtown Train' from the album *Hometown Girl* (Columbia, 1987)

Marianne Faithfull: 'Strange Weather' from the album *Strange Weather* (Island, 1987)

Patti Smythe: 'Downtown Train' single (CBS, 1987)

The Bobs: 'Temptation' from the album *Sing The Songs Of...* (Rhino ,1990)

Maura O'Connell: 'Broken Bicycles' from the album *A Real Life Story* (Warner Brothers, 1990)

Rod Stewart: 'Downtown Train' from the album *Downtown Train* (Warner Brothers, 1990)

Bulletboys: 'Hang On St Christopher' from the album *Freakshow* (Warner Brothers, 1991)

Screamin' Jay Hawkins: 'Ice Cream Man' from the album *Black Music For White People* (Demon Records, 1991)

Heavy Metal Horns: 'Way Down In The Hole' from the album *Heavy Metal Horns* (Square Records, 1991)

Nanci Griffith: 'San Diego Serenade' from the album *Late Night Grande Hotel* (MCA, 1991)

Bob Seger: 'Blind Love' and 'New Coat Of Paint' from the album *The Fire Inside* (Capitol, 1991)

Everything But The Girl: 'Downtown Train' from the album *Acoustic* (Atlantic Records, 1992)

Astrid Seriese: 'Yesterday Is Here', 'Little Boy Blue' from the album *Eclipse* (Netherlands, 1993)

Rod Stewart: 'Tom Traubert's Blues' from the album *Unplugged... And Seated* (Warner Brothers, 1993)

Astrid Seriese: 'Dirt In The Ground', 'Underground', 'Blow Wind Blow' from the album *Secret World* (Netherlands, 1994)

Shawn Colvin: '(Looking For) The Heart Of Saturday Night' from the album *Cover Girl* (Sony, 1994)

The Ramones: 'I Don't Wanna Grow Up' from the album *Adios Amigos* (UNI/Radioactive, 1995)

Bim Skala Bim: 'Train Song' from the album *Eyes And Ears* (BIB Records, 1994)

Rod Stewart: 'Hang on St Christopher' from the album *Spanner In The Works* (Warner Brother, 1995)

Bob Seger: '16 Shells From A Thirty-Ought Six' from the album *It's A Mystery* (Capitol, 1995)

T-Bone Burnett: 'Time' from the album *T-Bone Burnett* (MCA, 1996)

FILM APPEARANCES IN AN ACTING ROLE

Paradise Alley (1978) – Directed by Sylvester Stallone
Plays Mumbles the piano player
Wolfen (1981) – Directed by Michael Wadleigh
Cameo as inebriated piano player

One From The Heart (1982) – Directed by Francis Ford Coppola
Cameo

The Stone Boy (1982) – Directed by Chris Cain
Plays petrified man in carnival

The Outsiders (1983) – Directed by Francis Ford Coppola
Cameo as Buck Merrill

Rumblefish (1983) – Directed by Francis Ford Coppola
Plays Bennie

The Cotton Club (1984) – Directed by Francis Ford Coppola
Plays Irving Stark

Down By Law (1986) – Directed by Jim Jarmusch
Stars as Zack

Ironweed (1987) – Directed by Hector Babenco
Plays Rudy

Candy Mountain (1987) – Directed by Robert Frank
Plays Al Silk

Bearskin: An Urban Fairytale (1989) – Directed by Ann Guedes
Plays Punch & Judy Man

Cold Feet (1989) – Directed by Robert Dornheim
Plays Kenny

Mystery Train (1989) – Directed by Jim Jarmusch
Voice of radio DJ

The Two Jakes (1990) – Directed by Jack Nicholson
Cameo as policeman

At Play In The Fields Of The Lord (1991) – Directed by Hector Babenco
Plays Wolf

The Fisher King (1991) – Directed by Terry Gilliam
Cameo as Vietnam veteran down on his luck

Queens Logic (1991) – Directed by Steve Rash
Plays Monte

Bram Stoker's Dracula (1992) – Directed by Francis Ford Coppola
Plays R M Renfield

Short Cuts (1993) – Directed by Robert Altman
Plays Earl Piggot

Mystery Men (1999) – Directed by Kinka Usher
Plays Dr Heller

Cadillac Tramps (2000) – Directed by Thomas Sjölund
Plays adversary of gangster

THREE

THE LEGACY

Round about now, in a parallel universe very far from here, platinum songwriter and former jazz stylist, T Alan Waits, is sitting around a Southern California swimming pool with his pal Tim Rice. They cluck and chuckle over the minutes from the last ASCAP meeting. For a lark, Tim flips on an advance CD from avant-garde tone poet Diane Warren. Waits wonders briefly, What happened to the nice songs she used to write back when he knew her in the 1970s? But who cares? There is a more important question: how is he going to find the time to spend all the cash piling up from yet another Grammy-winning Song of the Year, the chart-topping 'The Me Inside of Me', written for his muse, Celine Dion?

It sounds at least as plausible as the reality we live with. Young Tom Waits started off in a bohemian fashion, a colourful and substantial lyricist with an arresting public persona, a thing for speakeasy drawlings over jazzy brushes and a Beat piano. But underneath, his songs were timeless and beautifully fashioned. Accessible, most certainly. His songs were covered by country-rock royalty, The Eagles, by soon-to-be-deceased folk hero Tim Buckley, and later by the Princes of All Rock, Bruce Springsteen and Rod Stewart. One would think the accessible part of him would win out, that the artist would even out, shave off the soul patch, work on a common vocabulary, and say hello to the commercial success that surely awaits him. Most popular musicians follow this path.

Take, for example, 'Roxanne', the early Police single. It sounded somewhat unorthodox when it came out in the late 1970s. Although the musicianship was sophisticated, definitely not punk rock, and although they weren't the first white band to play an adaptation of reggae, the straining of that distinctive voice against a stark background made quite a daring statement at the time. Now Sting and his music, although still distinctive and still sophisticated, are such a part of the popular consciousness that sometimes one forgets what he does for a living. The same goes for U2, once a furious little new wave bar band, and the great Bryan Ferry, who once wobbled around wearing eyeshadow whilst Brian Eno played with Joe Meek's sound effects library in the background. Becoming part of the cultural and commercial mainstream does not, per se, signal a deterioration of quality, but it does bring a softening of edges.

Compare Tom Waits: despite being a highly successful musician, not to mention film and stage actor and composer, Waits himself has never had a commercial hit. Starting off somewhere towards the populist end of the cult continuum, his music actually became more eccentric. And then still more so. Thirty years after the release of his first long-player, a striking yet still-identifiable example of a singer-songwriter at his craft, he put out *Black Rider*, a Germanic 'cowboy operetta' filled with stomping boots, pots and pans, and the winsome guest vocal of America's swingingest senior citizen, William S Burroughs. Nobody blinked. Neither did it stop Waits' career dead. The next album, admittedly a more hummable creation, went on to become the biggest selling independent album ever, winning *Mule Variations* a Grammy for Best Contemporary Folk Album in 1999.

Mick Brown, writing for *Vogue* magazine, commented charmingly that Waits' albums 'gave the appearance less of being released than of having escaped'. Waits himself says he doesn't think he takes *enough* risks. He began in the 1970s as a beatnik eulogizer of urban and badly-lit downmarket Americana. In the 1980s, he had a period of blues transition – the Captain Beefheart kind, of course – before his work took on a very European, theatrical style. Curiously, in both instances, he seemed drawn to the musical expressions of half a century ago. His work in the 1990s brought Europe back to America in brilliant and memorable fashion, with a country-blues engine driving a wacko German puppet show through shining fields of grunge.

If Tom Waits did nothing else, rock trombone players will always thank him for making them hip and useful again. When new wave and punk bands had run their course in the early 1980s, they generally had two options. They could go stadium rock, or they could take advantage of a newly affordable and fast developing music technology and go Euro-electronic or dance. Those who wanted to do neither were stuck with folk. At the time, few ex-punks were brave enough to cope with the stigma associated with folk music at the time, that of depressing shoes and student activists with beards. When Waits released *Swordfishtrombones* with its wonky brass instrumentation and prison-camp kick drum, he gave new options to countless musicians, and great validation to those who were that way inclined to begin with. He made an astoundingly inventive record by invoking the imagery of a bygone technology, the mechanical age of hand-cranked pianolas and clockwork drummers. He didn't just widen the musical vocabulary of rock, he drove right through the walls and staged a polka contest in the ruins.

There are only a handful of artists who began as fairly mainstream pop entertainers, and who ended up in a much more cult-like domain. Scott Walker's journey is surely the most dramatic, going from Top Ten crooner of lovely pop songs in the mid-1960s to unfathomable post-Brel hermit in the 1990s. The other would be Marianne Faithfull. In the 1960s she applied her girlish vibrato to folkie, English numbers written by Mick Jagger, and now she performs gritty, world-weary rock cabaret songs to a smaller, but no less appreciative audience. One would have to look to the field of classical composition to find more examples. It is interesting to note that both Scott Walker and Marianne Faithful, when they trekked off to the outer rings of rock, found comfort in European theatrical idioms.

Tom Waits doesn't seem too impressed by his own legend. He once told *The Face*'s Elissa Van Poznak that he was searching for a stand-in: 'all you need is a deep voice and a bad haircut'. He offered a salary and benefits ($125.00 plus vacation. This was 1987, and, presumably, a joke), to anyone willing to impersonate him at concerts when he had a conflicting engagement. He is notorious for making up unlikely stories about his past and his character. But this strange ambivalence does not extend to his art and its integrity. He successfully sued a company who used a Tom Waits impersonator in a commercial for potato chips, and he sought to prevent his former record label from releasing his earlier work. Most tellingly, he has also said that he couldn't laugh at the movie *Spinal Tap* because it was too real.

He is both pre-modern and post-modern, but never just plain

modern. Underneath, he is a conservative songwriter, a soft-shoe shuffling crooner who happens to gargle with broken glass and lighter fuel. If you listen to Waits singing 'The Piano Has Been Drinking', you can almost hear Gene Kelly taking a woozy stroll through the puddles on the way home. As the song comes to a close, you hear the voice fade: 'The piano has been drinking, not me... not... me... '. Around about this point, a kindly police officer would say to Gene Kelly, 'Move along now, fella.'

Waits has acknowledged that the artists who first influenced him were the pop balladeers of yesteryear like Perry Como. He has cited Bob Dylan as his lone contemporary inspiration, and an oft-quoted Waits-ism is that his reading was 'limited to menus and magazines'. One suspects this might not be so, and that the phrase's alliteration, rhythmic cadence and Naugahyde overtones pleased him more than the truth. Despite off-kilter, sometimes discordant and terrifying arrangements, the centre of Waits' music is purely musical. His lyricism is without peer, his easy melodic sense a gift to singers. At heart, he is an Old Time songwriter who has chosen to add spoken-word and eclectic soundscapes to his repertoire.

When pop artists draw on the past, they rarely go back further than the 1920s and the Jazz Age. Turn-of-the-century vaudeville and its precursors, the museum shows and the burlesque shows, lack the required youthful verve. Typically, Tom Waits has a profound obsession with the imagery of this pre-vaudeville era. The museums of the mid-1800s were a distinctly American diversion, a blend of freakshow and variety performance. Curio Halls displayed, in the guise of scientific education, nature's more unusual and dramatic variations, whilst later, on a cramped stage area, some kind of live entertainment would take place. This was considered family-oriented fun. For the gentlemen who just wanted to drink and look at women with two legs, there were the 'Tights Shows', which later became burlesque. Waits was born a century too late. He began as burlesque man, and ended up a museums man.

Theatre is an integral part of Waits' presentation. Rock theatre has always had a somewhat dubious reputation. The panicked spectre of the art school mime haunts the David Bowie of the late 1960s, when he was hanging out with Lindsay Kemp. Then there is the more deadly 1970s version, which began auspiciously enough with the extravagantly innovative Genesis, but soon lost all control. People went berserk with lightshows, dry ice and magician's robes (hello, Rick Wakeman). The only way it could end was with the advent of *Spinal Tap*. What hope for the 1980s? Thank heavens for *Swordfishtrombones*. The theatre here is evocative of Weimar Republic Germany, minus the overt political mummings; simple and personality-oriented. There may be contraptions and devices, but there's no laser show nor gated reverb on the drums. These days, Tom Waits has been known to perform with a few stage props, some piles of dust and a bag of cellophane confetti, but he is unlikely to end up either trapped in a mechanical pod (as did the unfortunate Derek Smalls in *Spinal Tap*) or flown across a howling auditorium in the manner of Garth Brooks or Tinkerbell.

The trend for singer-songwriters in the 1970s was towards a confessional, intimate writing voice. In contrast, the song tradition of mid-twentieth century continental Europe, popularized in France by Belgian-born singer-songwriter Jacques Brel, involved a more remote dramatizing of experience. Although Waits was a narrative writer, he has said that in his early days, he was too much in his songs. He may have been referring to his lifestyle, in the sense of living the songs, as much as to his writer's voice. He seemed to straddle both worlds throughout his career. His dramas are compassionately painted, far from the Gallic melodrama of Brel and his cabaret chums, the agonized descent into decadence and the torrid social protest, a style that sometimes veers towards camp. Waits, though given to wit, ironic flamboyance and the occasional bout of bad eyeliner, is not at all camp. He does strive for the authenticity of the theatre experience, and is much more northern European than Mediterranean in his approach. He has been frequently described as a 'post-apocalyptic' performer, the leader of the band playing in the blitzed ruins of the world. It's a true picture, but not necessarily a bleak one, in the sense of death and nuclear winter. It's more the idea that he improvises with what he finds in the ruins, finding Teutonic bossanovas in the debris of the shattered old order.

In a previously referenced article for *Vogue* magazine in 1987, Mick Brown identifies Waits as chronicling a uniquely American melancholy, the disenchantment under the bravado of American life. Waits has embraced the post-dustbowl America of John Steinbeck and the slang-laden, streetwise characters of Damon Runyon, and has combined this with the post-Kerouac beat poetry of later years. He has cited the existence of a 'common loneliness' that stretches the breadth of the United States. When questioned by Gil Kaufman and Michael Goldberg in an interview for ATN about the source of his characters, Waits replied, 'Trade secret… they're just plain folks.' He said they were both people he'd met and lived around, and people he'd heard of. In the early days, he had something of a reputation for writing about lowlife and being drunk, whereas in reality he wrote some oddly sentimental songs about prostitutes, gangsters and cocktail waitresses, which isn't necessarily the same thing. It's just plain folks. As for the alcohol, this serves to amplify the text, to open up the singer's heart and hold a mirror up to us all. In the words of the circus characters from the movie *Freaks*, (surely present in the T Waits home video library), 'One of us, one of us!'

When *Swordfishtrombones* was released in 1983, it was heralded as a breakthrough change of style, not just for Waits, but for music in general, and was the first of a trilogy of albums (*Rain Dogs* in 1985 and *Frank's Wild Years* in 1987 completing the trio) that explored new themes. The musical trends outside of Waits' most singular world had reached a crossroads. New wave was looking for something to do with itself. Confessional singer-songwriters had either moved towards the profitable writing of power ballads, or, in the case of Randy Newman, alternated between advancing cynicism and cinematic soundtracks. Because of the three-year gap between the release of *Swordfishtrombones* in 1983, and its predecessor, *Heartattack And Vine* in 1980, it would, at first, appear that the artist took a break and developed a new way of voicing his art. But in fact, the change was gradual and already in evidence when *Heartattack And Vine* was released.

In an interview released to reviewers by Asylum Records to promote *Heartattack And Vine*, writer Stephen Peebles reported finding a changed man, both as an artist and individual. This was in September 1980 and Waits was working in an office at Zoetrope Studios, composing the soundtrack for Francis Ford Coppola's *One From The Heart*. He said the change came about because he was freed from constant touring, from the exhaustion and bad health that ensued. He finally had space to think. A small but symbolic change had taken place – his drummer had changed from using just brushes, and was now permitted to use drumsticks. *Heartattack And Vine* is often described as a blues-oriented album. It starts to lean towards the surreal delta blues approach taken by Captain Beefheart on his classic album, *Trout Mask Replica*. Waits' later work continues to reflect Beefheart's sensibilities. Waits' first manager, Herb Cohen, also managed Frank Zappa, Beefheart's confederate in wackiness. In the Six-Degrees-of-Herb-Cohen kind of way that seemed to link every left-field artist in California, Tom Waits did have a vague association with Captain Beefheart, but it was more a parallel than an interactive connection. He was probably influenced to some degree by Beefheart, but then again, if Waits just decided to go for a harder, more bluesy sound, it would've probably come out as it did anyway, with or without *Trout Mask Replica*.

In addition, his romantic relationship with beatnik twin Rickie Lee Jones had ended and he had moved out of the self-imposed seediness of the Tropicana Motel. His move away from his old approach to music was probably very therapeutic, and his move away from the hipster's high life allowed him to step outside the jazz genre. It would seem that quitting touring and easing up on his drinking had slowly allowed the crammed memories of his youth to decompress and stagger out into the light, the images disoriented and inappropriately partnered.

Later in the decade, in a lengthy interview sent to reviewers accompanying the release of *Frank's Wild Years*, Waits addresses the change again: 'In some way, acting and working in films has helped me in terms of being able to write and record and play different characters in songs without feeling like it compromises my own personality or whatever. Before I felt that the song is me and I have to be in the song. I'm trying to get away from feeling that way, and to let the songs have their own anatomy.' In 1980, he found himself working at Zoetrope Studios every day for eighteen months. Coppola called *One From The Heart* a 'lounge operetta' and this new environment marked yet another opportunity for Waits to broaden his work. He had already written 'On The Nickel' for the Ralph Waites movie of the same name. An alternate version of the track appears on *Heartattack And Vine*. The roots of the change go back even further; in 1978, Waits took his first acting role in a feature film, *Paradise Alley*, the first of many movie appearances.

The delay in releasing *Swordfishtrombones* was a result of Elektra having declined to release it. Waits found Chris Blackwell's Island Records to be a more appreciative home. The album was recorded in August 1982 and featured some arrangements by Francis Thumm. You can still hear the underlying twelve-bar structure of the songs, but the instrumentation is quite a different matter. Thumm had worked with Harry Partch, a musician and composer who designed musical instruments from items he found whilst wandering the streets and backroads of America in the 1930s and '40s. Waits, who began songwriting by writing down the conversations he chanced to overhear at work as a bartender, was very sympathetic to the approach of found sound, and to instruments made of non-traditional components. Found sound was not a new concept by any means – but this was the first time that someone so established (by now, Bruce Springsteen had covered one of his songs) had introduced the notion.

The final key to the change is probably of most importance to the artist. Whilst working at Zoetrope, he met and married the projects script editor Kathleen Brennan, herself a writer and artist. Private and discreet, the most un-Yoko of rock wives, she stays behind the scenes of their many collaborations. Waits has commented that she is a voracious and adventurous reader, and that she keeps him informed of all the unlikely facts that fuel his work. He has said that many small decisions led up to his change of direction, but it appears that his partnership with Kathleen gave him a secure place to leave himself behind.

The *Swordfishtrombones* trilogy, Waits has said, was him exploring the 'hydrodynamics of his own peculiarities'. His work from here onwards is crammed with images of childhood, his own and those that all children hold in common, from music, storybooks, playground chants and nursery rhymes, and from films and events that they didn't fully understand when witnessing them. In 1985, he told the *New Musical Express'* Gavin Martin that the events of childhood, 'the way you perceive them and remember them in later life' had a significant effect on his writing. It's the way they are remembered that is significant, it is a most special distortion of perspective, and one that he seems to have retained. As a child he thought songs were not written but that they 'lived in the air'. This is such a wonderful concept. Waits is oftentimes, in his work and film roles, a throwback to a creaky, pre-moving-pictures world of childhood, a world of sinister wheezing pipes and upside-down *Chitty Chitty Bang Bang* loopy Victoriana. It is not so much nightmarish as just free from learned logic. It is certainly not infantile or sentimental, resembling more the nonsense poems of Edward Lear bumping up against the exotica of 1950s kitsch, *Bali-Hai* and the 'House of Bamboo'. It comes as no surprise to hear that Waits co-wrote a play, *Alice*, inspired by the story of the young girl who was Lewis Carroll's model for his famous fantasy, *Alice In Wonderland*. Both *Bone Machine* and *Mule Variations* have a crude, mechanical feel, as if one had come upon a cavernous, secret mine, manned by hip elves and fairytale streetwalkers. One suspects as a youngster, Waits was moved by the song 'Big John', fretted over the big man with the big heart, buried forever down a mine, and resolved one day to write some nice companions into Big John's sad tale.

Waits is moved by the sad sounds of inanimate objects, the beauty in the sadness and dignity of everyday people. He has spoken of abstaining from listening to music so that when he returns to it, he hears the ghosts in the machine, the subtext of the fourth dimension. One aspect of Waits that gets overlooked because of the high eccentricity content of his public persona is his contribution to world music. Though he has never really worked with musicians from other cultures in a Peter Gabriel kind of way, his sensibilities and his awareness of how, for instance, a banjo, with a slight twist of the tuning and timing, can go from Appalachia to Indonesia, have brought this global, un-rock approach into a harder-edged musical world. He once noted that a key factor in his approach was cultural incongruence; if you hear a music in its native environment, you really don't notice it. However, when you juxtapose an alien music in that same environment, there is a magical synergy. Waits observed that the tape machine was the same as a camera, in that some things that went in were magically improved and other things were lost. His is an almost mystical approach. He thinks that most songs don't like to be captured on tape, that they prefer their wild state, and that those he does hunt down tend to find their own logic. Waits' delight in this process is apparent in an anecdote he tells about his wife, Kathleen. She apparently misheard the words of the refrain of Creedence Clearwater Revival's 'Bad Moon Rising' as 'there's a bathroom on the right'. Waits points out, quite rightly, that when you go into a club, more often than not, there it is: the bathroom on the right.

In recent years, Waits seems to have become increasingly affected by northern European folklore. His collaboration with playwright Robert Wilson, released on CD as the album *Black Rider,* bears witness to this. It is fitting that this part of Europe has also provided Waits with his most feverish fan base outside of the USA, owing to their appreciation of Waits' unique reading of Americana. He has acknowledged that he was influenced by the songs of Kurt Weill, and if you listen, you'll see he bears more than a trace of Lotte Lenya in his phrasing. Lenya, who was married to Weill, was renowned as an interpreter of song during the German inter-war Weimar Republic era. Together with librettist Bertolt Brecht, Weill had his biggest commercial success with a rewriting of an eighteenth-century musical, *The Beggars' Opera*. Retitled *The Threepenny Opera*, it became a national obsession in the Germany of the late 1920s. Later, Weill and Lenya moved to the USA to escape Hitler's attentions, and the operetta was revived, to great success, on Broadway in the 1950s, with Lenya in a starring role. Waits seemed to have tapped into the same transatlantic consciousness that sustained Weill and Lenya.

Although Waits gave up his drunk drama when he left the early 1970s behind, he still maintained his connection to outsiders of all kinds. He is, being without peer in his musical field, something of an outsider himself. He began celebrating the lives of the great minority of losers and down-and-outs, melancholics and hookers, before moving on to the true outsiders of current society – scary neighbours and the so-called freaks of circus and carnival. In the days before rock 'n' roll provided a safe haven for alienated young rebels, the carnival was home to many a young outcast who never made it as far as the merchant navy.

Waits has brought the spoken word out of jazz and into the arena of rock, and has linked the jazz and blues of the 1930s and 1940s, and the beat poetry of the 1950s and 1960s, to contemporary folk music. He has a clear empathy for his fellow man, his chronicling of the oddness and the errors of humanity are painted with affection, free from judgement and/or distaste. His more theatrical work in the 1980s, beginning with the operetta-style *Frank's Wild Years*, has been a logical progression of the narrative yet poetic structure of his songs. He has put himself above categorization, unless you count 'Tom Waits' as a category in itself.

Waits' early work embodies a fine range of other voices. He told Gavin Martin, 'It's good to borrow, it implies you're gonna give back'. The hip blending of jazz and poetry had several fathers. Slim Gaillard's jive esperanto, a slang he termed 'Vout-O-Reenee', is especially apparent in Waits' work around the *Nighthawks* period. Gaillard was a man whose life story reads like he was invented by Tom Waits: born in Cuba, 'left' on the Greek island of Crete at age twelve, driver for the Purple Gang, boxing champ, recipient of a Purple Heart in the Second World War and inspirational figure for both Miles Davis and Jack Kerouac. Then there was Richard 'Lord' Buckley, the man who inspired Lenny Bruce, an American hipster given to wearing a pith helmet and affecting a last-days-of-the-Empire English accent. The 1950s saw jazz and poetry leave the bars for the coffee shop, where Allen Ginsberg read his Beat Poetry and the mellifluous bass tones of Ken Nordine brought forth his much-loved Word Jazz, a more whimsical, free-associative child of Beat. In his songs and singing, Waits carries traces of Stephen Foster, Woody Guthrie, Leadbelly, Howlin' Wolf, Wild Man Fischer, Bing Crosby, Louis Armstrong, Agnes Bernelle and a little shot of Lee Hazlewood, just to mess you up. A sterling cross-section of American song.

His career has a couple of notable parallels. David Thomas, formerly of Pere Ubu, has mined a cultural seam even further removed from reality than the one tended by Waits. Both share a susceptibility to Beefheart-itis. David Byrne, former Talking Head, does not, but he has, like Waits, collaborated with Robert Wilson and takes a similarly eclectic approach, albeit using modern-day technologies to do his bidding.

Beatnik princess Rickie Lee Jones and Tom Waits were more or less peers. They met at the Troubadour. As a singer-songwriter, Jones has a unique voice and was a startling influence on the hugely successful female songwriter/performers of the 1990s. Hear her all over Sheryl Crow's *Tuesday Night Music Club*, in the stream-of-consciousness pop confessions of Alanis Morrisette and in Jewel's folk-jazz vocalese. Jones' first album didn't debut until 1979, although her back view did grace the cover of *Blue Valentine*. By that time, Waits had released six albums and was moving out of his late-night beat poet phase.

German-born cabaret singer Ute Lemper has shown to great effect her sense of where Waits lies. On her album *Punishing Kiss* released in Spring of 2000, she performs songs not only by Waits, but also songs written by Scott Walker (impenetrable, inscrutable), Elvis Costello and Nick Cave, the latter two artists both avowed members of the Waits Brotherhood. Singer Holly Cole released an entire album of Waits' songs in 1995. The collection, entitled *Temptation,* was greeted with critical praise, and more tellingly, with great approval by many of Waits' fans. The artists himself has commented that when the great Johnny Cash covered one of his songs, 'That felt particularly validating'.

Any post-bohemian ne'er-do-well with a rumpled suit, a tale to tell, and a friend who plays the violin Turkish-style should stop a while and thank Mr Tom. Step right up The Violent Femmes, Stan Ridgway, The Pogues, Tindersticks, The Eels, Gavin Friday and David Johansen of The Harry Smith Project. Waits' defiant lo-fi recording techniques have also found great favour amongst a new generation of artists.

Waits has expressed an admiration for Prince, interestingly the only other popular artist who truly captures the creative spirit of our hero. There are some obvious, superficial differences, including musical style, shoe preference and, if you insist, chart positions. However, they share an artistic independence, an unprejudiced ear, and a determination to follow their muse, regardless of the commercial consequences. Both have a unique voice and adventurous spirit, yet both are popular artists with a cross-cultural appeal. Waits' fan base, as his live shows testify, stretches across several generations. Two of his three most recent albums (*Bone Machine*, in 1992, and *Black Rider*, from 1993) are his most abrasive albums ever, and almost ten years later, they still sound contemporary. Waits' music is not about the state of the industry or the art. It is about where the art has always been.

INDEX

PICTURE CREDITS

Picture section page 1: Michael Ochs Archive/Redferns. 2 top: Richie
Aaron/Redferns; bottom: Richie Aaron/Redferns. 3 top: Ebet Roberts/Redferns;
bottom: Liaison. 4 top: Gems/Redferns; bottom: Fin Costello/Redferns. 5 top:
The Ronald Grant Archive; bottom: Liaison. 6 top: Liaison; bottom: Ebet
Roberts/Redferns. 7: Perou/Time Out/Camera Press. 8: Paul Bergen/Redferns.